Ask Nana Jean *about...*

Making A Difference

Reflections on Life

by Jean Moule

Published by Skipping Stones, Inc.

Expanded Second Edition
$10

Making A Difference

About Nana Jean

Jean Moule was born in South Carolina and raised in New York City and Los Angeles. She earned her bachelor's from the University of California at Berkeley, where she studied art, psychology and education and was arrested in the Free Speech Movement.

While she and her forester husband raised three children, she earned a masters from the University of Oregon and a doctorate from Oregon State University. She is an emerita faculty member at OSU where she continues to teach about multiple cultures on-line and through the honors college.

Dr. Moule authored the textbook, *Cultural Competence: A Primer for Educators,* filled with many stories of schooling, some from her own family. She hopes that her work will help the nation's children, including her six grandchildren, to have culturally competent teachers.

Her words of inspiration come from her experiences and talks with her own children, grandchildren and friends. Visit Jean at **www.jeanmoule.com.**

Arun Narayan Toké, editor of *Skipping Stones* accepted Jean's first column and then encouraged her to share more on a regular basis. This work reflects both of our passions for multicultural understandings and our strong collegial relationship.

About Skipping Stones

Skipping Stones is a multicultural, literary, nonprofit, magazine that encourages cooperation, creativity and celebration of cultural and linguistic diversity in our youth. We explore stewardship of the ecological and social webs that nurture us. We offer a forum for communication among children from different lands and backgrounds. *Skipping Stones* expands horizons in a playful, creative way.
Subscriptions: Institutions: $35; Individuals: $25.
Overseas/Airmail Subscribers: *Add $15 for postage.*

Contact: *Skipping Stones*
P. O. Box 3939, Eugene, OR 97403 USA
E-mail: info@SkippingStones.org
www.SkippingStones.org
Publisher: **Skipping Stones**, Inc.

Table of Contents

Family

This 400 year old oak stands visible from our house and borders our garden.

From my own beginnings, to the love of my life, to stories of our children and grandchildren, this oak symbolizes where we are planted and how our lives have changed and grown over the years.

Nana Jean Reflects on Her Childhood

My grandchildren are beginning to tell stories and sing new songs. Their artwork often illustrates their favorite places. As they begin to use more words, I am planning to help them construct poems of their childhood. Perhaps you would like to write a poem, too.

Under each of the topics below, you list as many words as you like. Then you add some colorful adjectives or descriptions.

• Items found around your house • Items found in your yard • Items found in your neighborhood • Names of relatives, especially those that link you to your past • Sayings your family used/uses • Names of foods • Names of places you keep your childhood memories •

(This activity came from a May 2009 conference of the Oregon Chapter of the National Association for Multicultural Education in Salem, Oregon. We were given a worksheet to develop a "Where I Am From" poem. The activity was led by Professor Daniel Duarte using material by Linda Christensen of **Rethinking Schools**.)

Here is an example of what I wrote:

I am from the untouched, unused living room,

the stone terraza floors and too much TV.

I am from the manicured lawns fertilized by our Mexican-American gardeners

and the fig tree so big I could hide in the leaves high above the ground.

I am from a quiet city neighborhood, the playground

across the street and the one block I could roller skate around and around and around.

I am from the overworked, single mother, and the distant father.

I am from plenty of everything except family.

I am from a mother who could pass for white and a father who always wore a hat so that he wouldn't darken.

And, I am from a child who loved to spend time in nature and read the following book...and understood the experience.

The following excerpts are from **"I Wonder Why"** *by Shirley C. Burden (Doubleday, 1963), a picture book about a young Black girl's life experiences. Each statement is illustrated by a photograph.*

"I wonder why some people don't like me.

I like rain...and cool woods...

I like clouds floating in a blue sky...and birds...and cats...and little puppies.

I like the sea when it wears diamonds...and sand when it

squeezes through my toes...

I like flowers in spring...and lambs...and babies...

I wonder why some people don't like me."

Poems and stories like this help us understand why and how we experience the world around us. A special book we have enjoyed reading to our multiracial family is "**The Hello, Goodbye Window**" by Norton Juster *(Hyperion, 2005)*. In this book the Black grandmother is named Nanna and the White grandfather is named Poppy. It is good for my grandchildren to see a book that has grandparents that look like their Nana and Pops!

Nana Jean *On Love*

"The difference between an obstacle and a stepping stone is how high you lift your feet."

Love has many forms. In relationships, "unconditional love" allows each person to enjoy and appreciate others based on their very being, not their behavior. Teachers call this giving students "permanent value."

How has love held our family together? While faith is part of this bond, the love among members of our family has been expressed in unique ways. In 1964, my husband wrote:

> *"If I could live on grassy slopes,*
> *And see the world through pines,*
> *I'd culminate my fondest hopes,*
> *And build a home yours and mine."*

While we have built a physical presence, our efforts for a "family together means home," are more important.

When President Kennedy was shot in 1963, we were both attending the University of California at Berkeley. As the news swept the campus, many students found their way to the student union to listen to the broadcasts. In the midst of floor-to-floor solemn people, one man rested his head on a woman's torso. An art student at the time, I thought them an interesting picture and began to draw to pass the time and take my mind off the tragedy.

Some people may say of their beloved, "I loved you before I knew you." I can say to Rob, "I drew you before I knew you." Within days, through a dorm mate—the woman in the drawing—I met Rob (who soon became *my* Robbie).

I was smitten by Rob's poetry, which sometimes came daily. We hiked and enjoyed motorcycle rides around the Bay. After a few months I accepted his proposal that we be married the following June.

When we think of our early romantic days, one scene stands out. We were newlyweds, traveling to Salt Lake City to meet my father and his wife, before continuing by car to the East Coast for the rest of our honeymoon.

On the bus trip, we noticed a woman walking the aisles and talking to the other passengers. As she came even with us, I heard her say, "…and they even have the nerve to be wearing rings." We found out later that there was still a law on the books in Utah against interracial marriages.

We decided it was safest to wait in a dark movie theater until it was time to meet my parents. When we went to the hotel, we were told there was no record of a room reserved for us by my father. We then asked for my parents, who should have arrived. The clerk could not find their name on the register either.

We slowly walked out of the hotel with little money and no idea of how to contact my father in this hostile environment. On our way out, we glanced into the hotel dining room and saw my parents, eating and waiting for us.

My father went to the desk and insisted that we be given a room. He and his wife had had no problem registering because they were both Black. During our courtship and our marriage, this is the most blatant discrimination we have faced.

As a couple we like to travel, ski and spend time with our grandchildren. We're not sure, but we think part of the glue for our love is our determination to answer the naysayers to our marriage who inevitably said, "This marriage may work for you, but what about the children?"

When they were teenagers, one of our sons said, "If I tried to draw a picture of how much the two of you love each other, it would take a lot more hearts than what is shown on this card…I am very grateful to both of you for being together and for a solid family."

Our other son added, "…What is most important for me now is knowing wherever I am I can always come home or call home and find two loving and supporting parents. That number, two, is so important to me; people have told me they almost can't believe what a relationship the two of you have, and I realize how fortunate I really am."

These sons are in their 30s now, with children of their own. In December 2010, during a family visit, we were all around the dinner table when a blood clot entered Robbie's brain, causing a stroke that did not allow him to talk coherently. We had him at the hospital emergency room within eight minutes. Thankfully, he was given medication that relieved the blood clot, restoring his ability to talk.

Before Robbie was given the medication, he was asked to give his name, age, and tell where he was. He could not do it. Then the doctor pointed to each of our sons and asked him to speak their names. He could not do it. Finally, the doctor pointed to me, his wife of 45 years. Robbie looked into my eyes, and I could see him trying to get some words out. He could not say my name. A couple of words did come though: "my love." The emergency room crew collectively exhaled, and one son started crying.

This poem came from Robbie on a Valentine's Day: *"The Love we've shared since sixty-three*
Has grown beyond just you and me.
Our three beige babes have left the nest
And the years ahead may be the best."

Nana Jean: Encouraging Passionate Pursuits

When my children were the age of my grandchildren, a woman asked me, "What are their gifts?" At the time I did not know what to say, as I knew she was looking for a gift in music, art, dance, leadership or a passion for some facet of nature. I felt a little uncomfortable telling my new acquaintance that my children like to read, play Legos and talk. The reader became a lawyer, the Lego player an engineer and the talker a socially gifted teacher. Along the way, these passionate pursuits led to college majors and activities in line with their earliest interests. While many people eventually follow their "passion" in their life choices or play, many follow a more "practical" path in preparing for a career.

As an example, I pursued teaching as a career and have come only recently to following an early passion, drawing. I was aware of how I used my art background and aesthetic perceptions in everything from remodeling and garden designs to home decorating, yet a return to simple drawing has been extremely satisfying.

How have my children followed their early paths and how might my grandchildren follow theirs? In reading these connections do you see how your own path or those you care for may develop into a career that incorporates passionate pursuits?

My daughter, who read endlessly and climbed high up trees at age 5, was a competitive cyclist in college, while reading to her heart's content for a double major in English and history. She eventually completed a law degree and now climbs the subway steps in her urban environment and mountain trails when she can get away.

My son the Lego boy studied architecture and engineering in college and turned his active sports life into adventure racing and travel as he works as an engineering consultant in the USA and around the world. He continues to put together ideas and plans for the best of bicycle and pedestrian pathways.

My youngest son, the only child I know who did not go through a "No Strangers" stage around the age of one, could bring together a party in an hour as a teenager and does the same as an adult at his welcoming home. As a teacher, he leads middle school students and adults into amazing learning experiences.

And how have these gifts been transformed through connections with their life partners in the lives of the grandchildren?

My lawyer daughter married a socially-connected, precise individual with an extraordinary ear for language and music. I see their offspring having early gifts and passions that reflect this combination: both are bilingual and sing. The oldest has an eye for design, reads voluminously and revels in her athletic pursuits; the youngest connects many dots and ideas, while already showing strong leadership ability.

My engineer son married a woman with an eye for beauty and a strong sense of self. Their son is confident and already a strong cyclist at age 6. He had taken over 125 airplane flights by the time he turned 5.

The spouse of my teacher son has multiple gifts in music, drama, and leadership, as well as an ability to help others connect to what they need. Their son is off to engineering school, fluent in Spanish and especially kind to others. Their eldest daughter is already developing her artistic gifts and using them to perform. Their youngest daughter is learning Spanish, singing and of course, has Popsie (her grandfather) wrapped around her little finger. Her social gifts, reflecting both parents, are emerging in kindergarten.

Finding and Recognizing Gifts in Each

As an activity for yourself and those around you, why not make a list of your friends, family members and classmates and begin to list the gifts in each? Your list may begin with easily recognized ones: expertise in some area, gifts in fine or performing arts, noted leadership, creativity or the ability to make and connect friends. Consider character qualities such as dependability, flexibility or personality traits such as those who "love a challenge," or "ask penetrating questions."

The term "gifted" implies both giving and receiving and recognizes that the gifted person did nothing to earn it. Receiving a freely given gift may lead to a graciously accepted responsibility. Shouldn't gifts be used willingly in kindness and consideration of others? And shouldn't we have a willingness to share such gifts with the larger community?

Expanding Horizons with Nana Jean!

"…gee, I'm really happy I'm so far from town." This last line from a verse in a "Music Together" tape speaks to our need to get out of the city and see a bit more of the horizon. I am reminded of an essay, "Are you Rich, Are you Poor?" In this essay, a father took his son to visit a rural family in hopes that he would see poverty. Instead the son came home with a few reflections like this: "I saw that we have one dog and they have four. We have a pool that reaches to the middle of our garden and they have a creek that has no end. Our patio reaches only to the front yard and they have the whole horizon. We buy our food from supermarkets, but they grow theirs. We have walls around our property to protect us; they have friends to protect them." The boy's father was speechless. Then his son added, "Thanks, Dad, for showing me how poor we are."

Two of my grandchildren live well in Manhattan, yet they could use some of those expanded horizons. When shown a book with photos of New York City from the air they could easily identify Central Park, Metropolitan Museum of Art, Battery Park, Museum of Natural History and my favorite: "That's the Chrysler building near my Daddy's office!" But could they throw rocks in a river, or identify edible berries? In late June Jamie, 3, and Ainsley, 5, were without a babysitter, and their Mommy and Daddy decided that two months with Nana Jean and Pops, who live on four acres in rural Oregon, was a good solution.

We live in a clearing in a forest and while there is much to do, the children particularly *loved* our small ponds. One day Jamie and I were walking around the ponds watching little "skitter bugs"

From left to right: Chance, Jamie, Nana, Bella and Ainsley

darting around on the surface of the water. I told Jamie we needed a frog in the pond to eat those bugs. The next day I heard him talking to his older sister Ainsley as he looked at all of those bugs. He said, "Nana needs a **big** frog."

We were surprised to find that the mosquito fish had survived the winter, so we had an exciting time looking for them in the water and trying to count them. One day we decided to buy 40 goldfish for five dollars. Ainsley correctly suggested that we "release" the fish into the three ponds. Ainsley had to do the math on how to divide them. I think we decided on eight in each of the small ones and fourteen in the large one…wait, that is only 30…hmm…no wonder there were more than we thought! We put 39 goldfish in the ponds…the 40th did not even survive the ride home: he/she was duly buried, dug up and buried again…now with a marker on the island in the ponds. So, the children, as well as the two cats, spend much time looking into the water…where were those fish hiding?

One day they built a sand castle on the sand island in the ponds. Yes, the island has become a sandbox… not something I had planned on, but they were happy. The children helped to remove the algae that grew on the surface. Once, Jamie caught and released a goldfish. Some days the children went from PJs to swimsuit to PJs as they played in the sand, water and sun.

After getting tanned, with tough feet and lots of learning about gardening and llamas and forests and fish, Ainsley and Jamie flew home. As the last line of the song goes, "…gee, I'm really happy I'm back home in town."

Nana Jean: Cousins' Country Camp

Of the four grandchildren (from our three children) the oldest just turned 8, and the other three are very close in age—5, 6 and 6. They have lived very far away from each other: Florida, New York and Oregon. Because one of them is an only child and one has much older siblings, they really do appreciate spending time together as cousins. While holidays are fun, that usually only happens once a year…so Nana *(also known as Nannie)* and Pops *(also known as Popsie)*, decided to have a Cousins' Camp. *(Photo below shows the kids in their "Bird Camp" outfits singing a Chinese song).*

Each year, we have tried to match the focus of the camp with the ages of our grandchildren. We started with bunnies when the three youngest were around age one and moved to frogs when they were two. When they were three years old, our theme

was dinosaurs, then birds when they were four, and last year we chose insects as our theme. This summer the theme will be "sea creatures."

Each year, a seamstress makes them matching outfits: twirly skirts for the girls, reversible short pants for the boys, and t-shirts with the theme item on it. The camps used to be about four days long in the beginning and now they may be as long as three weeks.

We try to:

• See the actual creatures alive (for dinosaurs, there were very life-like creatures at a zoo exhibit). During the camps over the years, we have gone to see bunnies at the feed store, frogs around a lake where we hiked, and dinosaurs moving and roaring at the zoo exhibit. When we had the bird theme, we visited a nearby zoo where a Lorikeet exhibit allowed the children to feed the birds. We also had bird identification books with sounds for all the birds seen wherever we were.

For insect camp, we had three weeks: the first week was about insects in general and we had two books to identify anything that we caught. The second week, we studied and looked for arachnids and the third week we had emerging butterflies in a butterfly hatching kit.

• Find local camps that are related to the theme. For instance, at the local children's museum we found day camps on frogs and butterflies. Other things are worked in because they are available and we make them fit: an art camp, trips to the ocean, camping and hiking, and crafts, lots of crafts.

• Most years the children also work on a Cousins' Camp Production. This involves writing a skit, making costumes or parts of sets, choreographing, making and giving out programs.

Over time, my adult children have arranged their own vacations as couples during our Cousins' Camp when they know their children will be happily engaged.

Children spend many hours with Popsie in his garden, helping to plant, weed, water, pick, wash, cut and prepare fresh veggies, and of course, eat them! Every year, after the first time picking them, Chance wanted to dig up potatoes a second time. He also wanted to gather onions. They all love to pick berries.

The cousins who have been in Oregon in spring or early summer have helped in planting. Bella has planted onions, and Ainsley and Jamie, corn.

Pops says: "When they are here in the summer they can see the progress of what they have planted earlier. If they are here late enough, they can help harvest and eat."

The children have learned about and enjoyed natural foods and the enjoyment of gardening as well. Healthy memories!

Nana Jean: *Learning by Working Together*

Do you learn by having people tell you what to do? Or, do you learn from watching? I learned from my granddaughter how easy it is to gain skills and get information simply from working together with others.

A few years ago a former teacher of my children invited us to take part in a garden tour that raised money to help to restore a beautiful old house in our community. Not considering myself a true gardener and dreading the thought of getting ready for a couple of hundred people to walk on our property, I said no. After repeated requests, I finally agreed.

There is very little in life that will get one planning, working and gardening as much as being part of a garden tour. Almost everything else going on in my life was not as important as preparing for the tour, and my answer to any requests for other activities became, "Not now, maybe in July, after the garden tour."

One exception was when our son asked us to have our granddaughter, Bella, for the week before the tour. At age 7, she is more help than she is time-consuming. I learned an incredible lesson: my passion and depth of commitment for this tour translated effortlessly to her. Her mother said that after one week she seemed more mature. At the beginning of the week she cried and asked for her mother; but by the end of the week she confidently showed her mother and brother around when they arrived for the tour. She took them to the 20 stops on the walk around our place, showing them how we have a naturescape, which means that as we look at the plants and trees that grow naturally in this area, we encourage some, remove some, and add some.

She not only learned how to transplant tiny plants and memorized the common and Latin names of some plants, but also helped me note the tiny, identifiable flowers on native plants that had found homes on our land. Her presence as the native plant experts came to help us identify green things encouraged us all.

Her hands and legs saved mine as she ran to get tools and materials. She hauled buckets of weeds and dirt from the molehills that appeared each morning.

Bella likes to draw and letter. During the week she made the cutest signs, like one that hung on a high fence we called "Woodhenge." As people entered our property they laughed as they read her sign: *"Phlox: inside fence = nice phlox, outside fence = deer-eaten phlox."* Most of her signs were ones of caution: signs that said, *"Cats and Frogs Only"* kept people off some delicate bridges and walkways near our pond. And she helped me feel better about the dandelions I did not remove near one of the fences: *"WARNING! Do not pick dandelions, llamas will stick their heads out to eat them."*

"I have lots to do," she said before the tour began. She helped people find their way around, and she sold both her own and other people's plants at "Bella's Boutique." By the middle of the day she spoke of her fellow vendors as co-workers, referring visitors to them as needed and explaining what she was selling. She learned to smile, to share and to encourage others to take some of the plants home to their own gardens.

While I doubt that she will remember the Latin name of a dandelion, at least she knows it has one. She learned that plants need to move to larger containers as she saw the root-bound small tree she helped me replant. She knows that a smile and nice presentation will help sell goods. And she knows how much work goes on behind the scenes for such a tour. She learned by watching and working alongside of her "Nannie" and "Popsie," as she calls us.

Bella, instead of being a drag on my time, was the highlight of our tour and my most precious and wonderful memory of the day.

Nana Jean: Growing Focused Human Beings

While each of us is born into and becomes part of a culture, language and place, within those parts of our lives are many different opportunities that help us become unique individuals with unique contributions to our local and global communities.

I help my grandchildren make their way in the world with their passions through what I call the "Eight-Year-Old Trip." As each of my four grandchildren hit age 8, I identify some great and wonderful interest of theirs and take them on a trip to explore it.

By helping each one of my grandchildren become immersed in one of their interests, I hope to broaden their understanding. I also hope to give them viewpoints and language (both

Jamie at the Vivero (hatchery)

technically and linguistically speaking) that will help them pursue those interests as they grow.

When Ainsley turned 8, she had read J.K. Rowlings' series multiple times. The "Wizarding World of Harry Potter" had just opened at Universal Studios in Orlando, Florida. I flew from Oregon to New York City to pick her up, and we enjoyed three days of just Nana and Ainsley time. What a revelation! With only one youngster as a focus, we ate when she wanted to eat and did what she wanted to do! She grew up a lot in those three days: very little whining, and her clear requests were answered by me with a *yes*.

After Ainsley's trip, I began to wonder how to bond with and support Jamie. Jamie has talked about turtle conservation since age 4. Would his parents allow me to take him out of the country for **his** 8-year trip? Where could we go? His mother found reasonable airfares from NYC to Costa Rica. And we were off: first to find a suitable project, and then to make detailed plans.

We ended up at the "Refugio Mixta del Vida Silvestre Romelia" near Montezuma on the Nicoya Peninsula, an organization that protects olive ridley sea turtles as they hatch and crawl to the sea. It was an adventure into Jamie's interest and also into a unique surrounding culture. We used my very limited Spanish and his better Spanish to navigate the area and work through unexpected situations that arose.

Here is an example from my journal:

"Jamie and I are sitting at the hatchery *(vivero)* at 9:20 AM, 50 minutes into our 2 ½ hour shift. Fidel and Eoghan left, tired. They had been exhuming nests and digging the dirt out. The nests will air out for a day and then clean sand will be added in preparation for a new nest. When they were exhuming the nests, they found 21 little turtles. We watched two that were just coming out of the shell to complete their hatching. We felt the turtles probably would not survive or get to the surface without our help. There was one little hatchling that we had to help just a bit at the beginning of its slow but steady crawl towards the sea. As the water reached it, and it started to swim away with one flipper poking up on a stroke. Jamie said, 'He waved goodbye to us.' Another time, as three turtles that he had named swam away, he said, 'Good life, Jamie! Good life, Fidel! Good life, Bob!'"

This trip certainly ranks as one of the top ten weeks of my life, and I am certain Jamie will never forget it either. One of the other workers on the project said, "He is ridiculously smart for his age. He knows so much. He uses many words that an eight year old shouldn't know, like 'endemic' and 'marsupial.' There will be something very wrong in this world if he does not become a biologist or conservationist. The world needs enthusiastc people like him."

Two grandchildren have passed age 8, and there are two more to go. Chance likes to bike, hike and climb. Perhaps a trip to Utah for canyoneering and biking? And Bella—Will it be her fluent Spanish? Ballet? Singing? People skills? We'll soon see.

Nana Jean: Family Connections

In July 2013, my husband of 48 years, Robbie, celebrated his 70th birthday. We live in Oregon, as do his two brothers and our son. Our other son lives in San Francisco, and our daughter lives in New York. To mark this special milestone in Robbie's life, I invited some knew him to an event at our home. Both sons and his brothers surprised Robbie that late sunny afternoon. We exchanged stories and took photos.

I had a brilliant idea: Why not go around the long table and ask each person how many years they had known Robbie and the nature of their relationships? There were both light comments, for example, from a couple who had only known him a week, as well as deeper connections from people who had known him for over 40 years.

At one point, Angela, my daughter-in-law, spoke. She said that when her father died a couple of years ago, Robbie told her that from then on he would be her father. Angela had two children before she married my son. We have tried to include Quinci and Jaylin in many of our close family times, though they are older than the rest of our grandchildren, who are often pictured with me on this page. Jaylin, at age 20 and in the middle of his undergraduate years in college, wrote a birthday note that brought tears down my cheeks:

Robbie, Happy 70th Birthday!

I hope it's an awesome one, and that this decade is full of love, adventure, and blessings. And who knows, you might even get some great-grandkids. You should know that I truly admire you, and hope to be as responsible, caring, and easygoing as you are when I grow up. I'm quite thankful to have you in my life.

Love, Jaylin

Family and love extend beyond those with biological connections. Thank you, Jaylin, for making it very clear.

With families spread across the country it is a challenge to spend time together. One way of connecting with our spread apart grandchildren is a yearly gathering of cousins. Our eighth year of the Cousin's Camp *(see Mar. - Apr. 2011 issue)* for the four grandchildren also brought their parents and other friends to our home for their annual program. This year's theme was "Plants." The kids dressed as a blackberry, a tree, a flower and a sword fern *(with a plastic sword)*. We gathered to watch the children play in their costumes and sing the lyrics to "Invasive Species in the House Tonight," "Planting Awesome," and "Popsie's Plants are Growing."

After the event, while the kids hugged the huge oak in our front yard, the strong women that hold our family together had a moment of closeness *(see photos)*.

Family trees include branches grafted in, and the life of love and good character results in the fruit the branches bear. As a networker and resource finder, I have been able to connect my grandchildren and others with skills within my family. While Great Grandmommy Mary Ann has the children for her grandmommy cooking school, my son taught in the teacher education program I worked with at Oregon State University. I have had the privilege of bringing my professional career and my family even closer when I co-taught an on-line class first with my daughter, a lawyer in New York City, and later with my daughter-in-law in Portland, a school principal. My other daughter-in-law, a meteorologist, can give me insights into the weather as I learn to fly. What a joy to have reasons beyond family to bring our expertise together for the good of others while enjoying each other's company!

—Jean Moule. Below: Daughter Mary; Daughter-in-laws, Jenn and Angela; me & mom, Mary Ann. Photos: Stu Chalupsky.

Nana Jean: *Cultural Connections*

My granddaughter, Ainsley in New York City, has a good friend named Octavia (see photo below). As I watched these two fourth graders practicing hurdles, I spoke to Octavia's mother, Asari Beale, about my column that helps bridge cultures. Asari began to tell me about Octavia's connections to another friend and how their worlds were both similar and different. Asari works with Reach Out and Read *of Greater New York, an organization that promotes children's literacy. She wrote the following story for this column.*

From Harlem to Chinatown

Octavia Beale squeezed her mother's hand as they climbed out of the subway station into the noisy streets of Chinatown. They had traveled there from their apartment way uptown in Harlem, to visit Octavia's friend Lauren. Though she had been there once before, she was still excited by the narrow winding streets cluttered with stores and restaurants and sidewalk vendors selling all kinds of fruits and vegetables. It was too exciting—being in a new part of town, and going to see her best friend—she yanked on her mom's arm and rushed forward. "Come on, hurry up! We're going to be late! Come on!!!"

"Slow down! We won't be late." Mrs. Beale knew this mood. When Octavia got excited about something, she could get as jumpy as a kitten in an aviary. Luckily, her mother knew just how to calm her down. She would distract Octavia with conversation.

"So," she began. "What is it that makes you and Lauren such good friends?"

"I don't know… Stuff. C'mon, mommy! The light is changing."

She pulled her mother across the street.

Mrs. Beale tried again, "Stuff like what?"

"Well… We both like building things and making up codes."

"That's true. What else?"

"We like to draw. We both like Harry Potter. Oh—and we both like to eat weird stuff, like rice balls and stuffed grape leaves."

"Those things don't seem so weird to me."

"Well, stuff other kids think is weird."

"I see."

Octavia was slowing down now, which was good.

Mrs. Beale's arm was already sore from all the pulling. She would need to keep the conversation going.

"I can think of something else you have in common," Mrs. Beale said.

"What?"

"You both live in ethnic neighborhoods."

Octavia thought about it a second. "Hey, that's true!"

Most of the people who live in Harlem are African or of African descent, and Harlem is known around the world as the center of Black American culture.

Octavia looked around. The busy storefronts and chatter of families in Chinatown reminded her of 125th Street in Harlem, where people came from around the city to shop, and where you could buy jewelry, books, and even African masks from sidewalk vendors.

Mrs. Beale went on. "And you both have grandparents from other countries."

"Yeah!" Octavia said. "Lauren's grandparents from her mom's side are Chinese…"

"And your *abuelo* and *abuela* are Panamanian. So you both have one side of your family that speaks a language other than English."

"I never thought of that before," Octavia said.

"Well, now you have. Hey, where are you going?"

Octavia looked confused. "To Lauren's apartment."

"But we're here."

Octavia looked up. "What? How did we get here so fast? We were talking so much, I didn't even realize…." She narrowed her eyes at her mother. "Mom, did you do that on purpose?"

Mrs. Beale shrugged. "What do you mean?" She hid her smile and held the door open. "Now, I know something you, Lauren and I all like: Lauren's grandmother's dumplings! I wonder if they'll have some for us."

"Let's find out!" Octavia shouted, and pulled her mother into the building.

Skin Deep

We are each born into the world with varying physical characteristics that influence how we are seen by others and how we see ourselves. These columns, written for and about my multihued children and grandchildren, may help us all as we grow from preexisting roots and relate to those around us.

Ask Nana Jean about Hair

My name is Jean Golson Moule. I was born in South Carolina. I moved to New York City with my parents and went to school in the Bronx when it was primarily Jewish. I was the only African American child in my classroom.

When we moved to Los Angeles, California, I went to very multiethnic/multiracial schools from second grade through high school. I have three children and six grandchildren. They all call me Nana. Here you see my four youngest grandchildren and my latest hairstyle. I now teach teachers at Oregon State University.

Many African-American women with long, dark, curly/braided hair get questions or comments like these: *How do you get your hair like that?, How do you get your hair to do that cool twisty thing?, Can I try braiding it, or twisting it?, or, Can I touch your hair?*

Often, we tell them, "Sure! Can I touch yours?"

My hair is huge; it's kinky, messy and untamed. It's very wild stuff. As a teacher, I am used to kids asking to touch it. Random adults also tend to ask to touch my hair. A fourth grade teacher told me, "I generally don't mind. After having an entire class of fourth graders run their hands through my hair, anything else goes!" With people I don't know very well, it isn't comfortable, but I say *"Yes,"* However, for many people this would be awkward at best, and offensive at worse. So say, *"I like your hair, may I touch it?"* Be polite, don't assume, think, "Would you like someone touching your hair, even when they ask you nicely?"

My hair grows this way. I wear it natural (I now wear it in locks). Sometimes, other Black people compliment me and inquire about where my locktician is located. Years ago, when I used to wear braids or twists, I'd get a few comments now and again from non-Black people. *Would you share your beauty secrets?*

I wash my hair with water and shampoo, like most people. But since I have locks, some kids and even adults assume I don't wash my hair. When White people want to grow locks, they have to let the oils build up in the hair so that it will lock. People with thinner hair can't wash theirs often or the locks will come out.

If someone asks me, *"How do you cut your hair?,"* I am tempted to say, "Scissors are good. How do you cut yours?" But I might simply answer: "At the barber shop or the beauty salon."

Some curious girls ask me: *How long does it take to do your hair?, or, Do you do your hair braids everyday?*

The initial braiding of the hair depends upon many variables, like the style of the braids, the skill of the braider and the thickness of the hair of the person receiving the service. Time investment ranges from two to ten hours for the braider to complete the task. Also, braids generally require daily maintenance.

If you ask questions like: *Why do you flatten your hair out sometimes?, Does that mean you don't think it's beautiful when it's curly and energetic and woolly?, or, Why do you change your hair so often?*

I may say, "because I like change. Because I can. Because it's fun." Some African American women straighten their hair for the look, manageability, pressure to conform or personal preference. Many, many others choose natural styles.

If you are seriously interested in African American hair, I recommend: **Hair Story:** *Untangling the Roots of Black Hair in America (Byrd & Tharps, 2001).* The book covers topics ranging from the management of Black hair in Africa during the 1400s, to the lack of choice of hair management during the times of slavery, to the choices of hair management in modern times.

Glossary

Locked hair: Also called dreadlocks, locks or dreads. They are matted ropes of hair which will form by themselves if the hair is allowed to grow naturally without the use of brushes, combs, razors or scissors for a long period of time. Although the term dread lock was originally associated with the Rastafarian community, people of various cultures have worn and continue to wear locks.

Locktician: Someone who specializes in the care of hair that is locked, may include initial locking, maintenance, and styling.

Summer's Coming! Ask Nana Jean about Swimming

Summer is coming and with it, opportunities to swim and play in the water. Nana Jean hopes you are safe near water, and that you will learn to swim if you have not learned already.

Amazingly, some people, because of their experiences, have questions about African Americans and swimming.

I have never seen an African-American in my neighborhood pool or on the Olympic Swimming Team. Can black people swim?

If you live somewhere that is highly segregated you may not have seen someone of African descent swim, so I understand that you may wonder if Black people can swim! Read the questions and answers below to help you understand why some Blacks do and some don't.

Isn't swimming like most things? That is, race has little to do with ability?

Yes, some African Americans can swim very well. Someone I knew laughed when I asked him if he could swim. He said, "Are you serious?.... Not only can I swim, I was a certified lifeguard at the age of 18 and have saved several individuals from drowning."

Does where you live make a difference on whether you learn to swim?

An African American woman told me, "In Inglewood, where I grew up, there were no pools in which to swim, no golf courses or tennis courts. Only basketball and track fields. I learned when I was 30 years old." Another Black friend told me, "I can swim; my brother was a junior lifeguard at the closest YMCA. It took us forever to walk to the pool in the summer because our poor neighborhood did not have backyard swimming pools or adequate funding for public facilities with pools. Even today, the parents of poor children do not have the disposable income necessary to pay for private swimming lessons."

What are other reasons people do not learn to swim?

My own mother, who is 83, never learned to swim. In her childhood, public pools had "Whites Only" signs.

Also, some religions require women to be covered well in public. However, there *are* companies that make swim suits that cover the whole body.

Shouldn't everyone learn to swim?

I think so. Some high schools or colleges require students to learn to swim. One person told me, "Yes, I can swim, but only because it was a requirement of my undergraduate degree. All undergraduates had to enroll and pass a swimming course."

Nana Jean, can you swim?

Swimming was a requirement in my high school and that's when I really learned to swim. The African-American girls, who usually had their hair straightened in those days, dreaded having the class first period. Just a little bit of water and we would have a bad hair day. I remember putting a thick layer of hair oil under the edge of my swimming cap in order to keep the water out and my straightened hair straight. I think some of us said we were beginning swimmers even if we were better than that just because then we would not have to put our heads under the water as much. But you had to pass the swimming test, or you had to take the class again. A lot of girls became better swimmers during the last week of class. So I would say that at the age of 15, I could sort of swim, but my hair couldn't!

Now, I wear my hair in locks and I really like to swim. I have swum across a lake, I have taken part in a triathlon (swimming, biking and running) and I have jumped into water with ice in it and swum a very short distance. Refreshing!!

How about you, reader? Can you swim?

Ask Nana Jean about Skin Color

Why are people different colors?

The tone of human skin can vary from a dark brown to a nearly colorless pigmentation, which appears pale pink due to the blood in the skin. Skin color is based on the amount of melanin[1] in the skin. In general, people who live near the Equator have darker skin and people who live far from the Equator have lighter skin because they have adapted to more or less exposure from the sun.

How do children learn about different color of skin?

I have a friend who tells the story of going to the bank with her daughter who lived in an all-White community. While holding onto her mother's hand, she stretches around to get a good look at the man in front of her from both sides and then says, "Look mommy, a chocolate man." In a situation like that, rather than telling the child she'd said something bad, she calmly explained that different people have different skin colors and that all skin tones are beautiful.

Until I was about eight years old, I didn't know about races. I thought everyone was the same. Mom was a lot lighter than we were and my sister was a little darker and younger than I was, so I figured that people's skin stretched as they got older!

One of my grandchildren describes her family members like this: "brownish, whitish, tan, honey."

Why do children learn to be afraid of people who have different skin tones?

It is hard not to get the idea that certain skin tones are more valuable in our country because of the way people of different colors are shown in the movies, advertisements and on TV. Also, parents may accidentally teach their children that certain skin tones are "scary." Babies begin to learn racism when they are just months old. For example, a White mother in an elevator is holding her five-month-old baby. A Black person gets on the elevator, and the mother tightens her grip. The baby experiences "threat" or "danger."

Have you ever had someone treat you badly because of the color of your skin?

Yes, many times, even now. Racism is not as open as when I was a child. When my sister and I were children, we went to South Carolina by plane and we had a stopover in Florida. We were *so* hungry and there was a hot dog stand about twenty feet from where we were sitting and mom wouldn't get us any food. She didn't have the heart to tell us that they wouldn't have served us because, at that time, some people would discriminate[2] against people with dark skin.

Is it like this in other countries as well?

In other places in the world, color of skin is treated differently. Sometimes worse and sometimes better. My sister told me, "When I was in Holland years ago, I noticed that the Dutch seem to be colorblind. It was so strange not to be looked at as a *brown-skinnned* person first."

Sometimes people think I am from another country because my skin is not White. What could I say?

The North American continent had brown-skinned people living here long before any White people came here. Except for the Native Americans, most of our ancestors were from other continents. So this person does not know history very well. I might answer this question this way: "I am from the United States of America with some ancestry from the continent of Africa. I have not learned the specific country,…yet."

My teacher sometimes mixes me up with my friend who is also Asian. What should I say?

Sometimes, when people look at people who are very different in skin tone from their own family and friends, they have a harder time telling people apart. When this happens to me, I usually just smile and tell them that I am not that person. It is very frustrating, but I think that kindness is the best response. You might say: "Oh, that was not me, I think I know who you meant though." Or "You must have mistaken me for someone else."

Why are your grandchildren all different colors?

Because my husband is White, some people would say that our children were going to be so "beautiful because mixed kids look cuter." It is better to use the term "multiracial." I think our children and our grandchildren are a beautiful range of color, I think all skin tones have beauty in them. How fortunate you are if you live in a place where you can see people of all different colors. ✥

[1]*Melanin is a colored pigment that is found in skin and hair. Melanin protects from sunburn.*

[2]*Discrimination based on skin color is called racism.*

Nana Jean: Are You White? Are You Black?

Are you White? Are you Black? Biracial children may hear this question. How do they respond?

Imagine a mother holding her newborn in her arms and noticing that the baby's skin color is different from her own. What is she thinking? How does she feel? My daughter-in-law said her first thought was, "Whose baby is that?" when her child with lighter skin-tone was born. When my first child was born, my roommates in the hospital room said, "Are you sure that is your baby?"

Now that baby can be identified in all her racial categories on the United States Census Form. It was not always this way.

My biracial daughter, my first child, was born in 1969. As an African American, I was surprised when the doctor who examined her when she was 7 weeks old listed her as "White female." Mary has been listed in 5 census reports now. In 1970, regardless of what the doctor said, I checked "Black" for her. In 1980, I asked her how she would like to be listed. At age 10, it was a difficult and emotional moment for her. Should she put "Black" like her mother? Or "White" like her father?

I must admit that after Mary was born I prayed, "Dear God, next time, I would like a little boy, with brown hair, and brown eyes, and brown skin." I know now that it makes Mary sad. I loved her very much with her wavy blond hair and blue eyes. At the time, though, I was the only person with brown skin in my church, my neighborhood, my town! In fact, according to the 1970 census, there were only 22 African Americans out of 72,000 people in my county! I wanted to hold a child that was brown like me.

In the 1980 census, Michael, the answer to that prayer, decided to check the "Black" Box. Mary checked off "White."

In the 1990 census, Mary identified herself as "Black."

Finally, in 2000, Mary had the option, if she chose it, of checking two different races on the census form.

In the 2010 Census, Mary *(see left)* and her husband, both biracial, checked just one box: "Black." And that's what they chose for their two children.

How do biracial and multiracial children feel about having parents of different skin tone?

Mary's first child, a girl, is of noticeably darker color than her parents and her younger brother. What does she think? She says her family is "brownish, whitish, tan, honey."

Regardless of parents' viewpoints on racial identity there are various, thoughtful reasons for thinking about race and racial identity in different ways in different families. For some people, there may be a need to identify a certain way because of the surrounding community. Family conversations about racial identity may or may not help with understanding your place in the community or the world. More important is gaining broad horizons and the self-confidence that allow children to figure these (and many other) things out for themselves. That may be much more important than an early exposure to multicultural identity.

And while race still matters in both small and large ways, it is my hope that someday Martin Luther King Jr.'s words will become true: "I have a dream that my four little children will one day live in a nation where they will not be judged by the color of their skin but by the content of their character."

It is easier than ever to appreciate the richness of having parents of two or more racial backgrounds now that our President is biracial. My hope is that "beige babies" will be increasingly appreciated and valued as part of our multi-ethnic, multicultural nation. The book, ***Shades of Black: A Celebration of Our Children*** (*Scholastic*) gives us a glimpse of these multi-hues called Black: *I am…creamy white…and silky smooth brown/ And…golden brown/ I am…velvety orange… and…coppery brown/ I am…radiant brassy yellow…and…gingery brown/I am Black. I am unique.*

Ask Nana Jean!... *About Biracial Identity*

What *race is presidential candidate Barack Obama?*

Barack Obama, the child of a Kenyan father and a white mother from Kansas, is an example of the many biracial, multiracial, multicultural, and multi-ethnic people who are born and live in the United States. As you can see from my photo, my grandchildren are of varying colors. When my husband, who is white, and I were married in 1965, he wrote me a poem about how our family would have beige babies.

Two of our biracial children married people who are also biracial (with one African-American and one white parent). Another generation of "beige babies!" So, how do "beige babies" help us? They may be able to identify with more than one group, and may be able to bridge racial, cultural, or language differences. They increase awareness for more mono-cultural communities of the multicultural nation and world in which we live. They may even be able to share hair-care and fashion tips with their friends from different cultures.

Many people have asked our children and other multiracial people "So, what are you anyway?" Each person may have a different answer, based on his or her own experiences. In this country, it used to be that biracial people didn't get to identify that way, but were assigned to the category that was not white. That concept, at least for individuals of mixed African ancestry, was called the "one drop rule," as in: "One drop of Black blood made you Black."

Nowadays, many people choose the race they want to identify with or choose to celebrate their multiracial heritage. Even the policies of the official United States census have reflected changing trends. The census has collected data about race since the first census in 1790. But the method of identifying race and the categories used have changed over time. Until 1960, official census-takers decided which category to put somebody into; and categories were assigned through a combination of direct interview and self-identification in 1960 and 1970. Since 1980, people have been able to select

a category for themselves. And in 2000, for the first time, individuals could pick more than one race.

You might be surprised to learn that only 2.4 percent of the population had reported two or more races in 2000. Researchers have shown that many more people have mixed racial ancestry including some people who identify themselves as white.

There are many reasons why people may choose to identify with just one group; perhaps to feel closer to that community, to honor a particular aspect of their heritage, or to influence policy decisions. Some people may have selected only one race on the census form because after years of following instructions to "check only one box," they didn't feel comfortable doing anything else.

However, that may be changing. People under the age of 18 were more likely to report more than one race in the 2000 census. Forty-one percent of people who selected more than one race were under the age of 18, while just 26 percent of the total population were under age 18. Today, many kids have heroes who have a multi-ethnic background, such as Barack Obama and Tiger Woods. In addition to showing us a picture of opportunity, hard work, or success in their fields, these individuals can teach us about different cultures and about the bridging role that multi-ethnic people can play.

A wonderful children's book, **"All the Colors of the Earth"** by Sheila Hamanaka *(published by HarperCollins, ISBN: 978-0-688-11131-1)* says it well:

Children come in all the colors of the earth—
The roaring browns of bears and soaring eagles,
The whispering golds of late summer grasses,
And crackling russets of fallen leaves,
The tinkling pinks of tiny seashells by the rumbling sea…
Children come in all the colors of love,
In endless shades of you and me…
Children come in all the colors of the earth and sky and sea.

Here is to our wonderful, multi-hued country.

Nana Jean *On Racial Identity in Children*

Growing up in a racially and culturally diverse community helps children develop a healthy racial identity. While "race" is not determined strictly biologically, people with different physical features, including different skin colors, do tend to be treated differently. Understanding how these differences affect how we think about ourselves and others is called "racial identity development." One way to think about racial identity is these four levels: I'm OK, You're OK; Something is Not OK; I'm OK, I am not so sure about you; and I'm OK, You're OK, We're OK.

In the first level, people try to ignore that skin color makes a difference in how people are treated. It is called being "Color Blind." It would be nice if that worked, if we could truly treat all people the same way. However, there are biases built into the advertisements we see, the images on television and the minds of people who are hired to work at different jobs. For example, when I was six years old, my family quietly moved into an all-white, mostly Jewish neighborhood. Despite an act of overt racism—one morning my father had seen "N——— go back to where you came from" scrawled on the outside of the house and, without telling anyone, washed it off—my parents had hoped that the school personnel would treat me like any other child. Perhaps pretending there was no difference would allow me to "fit in." My parents hoped that an "I'm OK, you're OK" attitude would be enough to ensure my safety and success.

Unfortunately, this did not happen, for race and culture did matter. I experienced being different even as I worked to fit in. For example, during a Jewish holiday, only two students attended school, and I was the only child in my classroom. I wondered, "Why isn't the teacher teaching me today? I am here!" Both in school and socially, I was often alone. This is an example of "something is not OK."

My phase, "Something is not OK," slowly progressed to anger and the "I'm OK, I'm not sure about you" stage. One day my mother came to pick me up early from second grade because the teacher said I waited at the door and stomped on the toes of my classmates as they left the classroom! My mother observed this.

The next year my family moved from our East Coast urban area to a West Coast suburb. My new school was as culturally diverse as any Los Angeles school could offer. Miss Thomas's room was a secure and healthy place for my own emotions and my classmates' toes. I was learning about my own culture alongside many others.

My teacher used strategies that seemed to validate every child in her room. Each day, Miss Thomas wrote a Spanish phrase in the corner of the blackboard. She read it to the class, then had the children repeat it. In less than a minute of classroom time, she acknowledged her Mexican American students and opened the door to another language for all her students. Her classroom was safe from disrespect toward her or among students. In this situation, as a result of a caring and skillful teacher, I entered into the "I'm OK, you're OK, we're OK" stage.

Understanding that each of us, whatever the color of our skin, moves through these levels in some manner may help us to accept and get along well with people with many kinds of differences.

—*Professor Jean Moule, Oregon State University.*
Below: Nana Jean's Fifth Grade Class Photo.

Nana Jean: *"Blink of the Eye" Racism*

In the blink of an eye, an unintentional bias was visible to me, an African American woman. A man saw my face as I walked into a store and reached his hand back to see if his wallet was safely in his pocket. On the street a women catches my eye a half block away and moves her purse from the handle of her baby's stroller to her side as she arranges the baby's blanket. What is happening here? Was it the sight of my brown face that caused these reactions?

I believe these are cases of "blink of the eye" racism: reactions resulting from unconscious negative feelings based on the color of skin. I don't believe it is possible to be raised in America without some feelings like this towards black or brown folks of any age. We usually do not personally choose these ways of seeing people. In fact we are usually not aware that we have such images in our heads. Such embedded feelings towards brown people seem to be in the air we breathe (not to mention the radio and TV waves). How sad, for we know that most people do not want to be considered capable of acting like this. How does it happen?

Racism and biases are rooted in stereotypes and prejudices. A stereotype is a simple image or twisted truth about a person or group based on a prior judgment of ways people act or their habits and abilities. Ethnic and racial stereotypes are learned as part of how and where we are brought up. A good example of this is a recent conversation that repeated a doll study from 1954. In a video taken in 2006 by a 17-year old film student, a young Black child describes a Black doll as looking "bad" and the White doll as "nice."

Children are a little less able to hide these different feelings about skin color. Sometimes, even when we say, "some of my best friends are Black," we may mean that "my best friend" is an exception to stereotypes and, therefore, other Blacks would *not* be my friends.

It is important to remember that we are designed to quickly figure out who is enemy, and who is friend. In the past—and certainly in many places in the world today—the ability to quickly identify friend or enemy may be a matter of life or death. People who respond to their gut reactions to my brown skin in surprisingly non-verbal ways may be quite gracious, if given another second or two. Recent brain research shows that while most people have an instant activity in the "fight or flight" part of their brains upon encountering an unexpected person or situation, a first reaction is often overridden in a nanosecond, allowing people to respond as their better, kind and accepting selves by overcoming built-in biases.

The first evidence of this unconscious bias came from insects and flowers. Dr. Anthony Greenwald drew up a list of 25 insect names and 25 flower names and found that is was far easier to place the flowers in groups with pleasant words and insects in groups with unpleasant words rather than the reverse. It was difficult to hold a mental picture of insects with words such as 'dream,' 'candy,' and 'heaven,' and flowers with words such as 'evil,' 'poison' and 'devil.' Greenwald then took the next step, using White-sounding names such as Adam and Emily and Black-sounding names such as Jamal and Latisha, and grouping them with pleasant and unpleasant words. Greenwald said that he had much more trouble putting African American names next to pleasant words than he did putting insect names with pleasant words.

Knowing that you have a feeling for or against a group may cause you to more carefully consider your responses and actions. How do we find a key to unlock this door to the mind? There is a test that has helped millions of people find out more about themselves. It is called the I.A.T. or Implicit Association Test. The ***Teaching Tolerance*** web site below can also help you to understand some of the words I have used: www.tolerance.org/activity/test_yourself_hidden_bias.

—*Professor Jean Moule, Oregon. For an in-depth version of this, please see her article in* **Phi Delta Kappan** *Vol. 90, no.5, Jan. 2009 (pages 320-326).*

Travels

Seeing the world from different perspectives and through different eyes opens our minds to ways of knowing as well as common human understandings and relationships. From the beaches of Mexico, to high on Kilimanjaro, to the devastated areas of New Orleans, I share my new understandings and viewpoints.

Cycle of Enlightenment

I have visited New York City a number of times in the last four years as my daughter is raising two of my grandchildren in Washington Heights, just north of Harlem. While I used to find the city dirty, and the people strange and distant, I have had a major transformation.

I now find the city wonderfully complex, the streets full of life, and the people amazingly friendly. For instance, not once did I have to carry my grandson-laden stroller up a long flight of stairs from the subway without someone, many ones actually, of all ages, races, genders, offering to lift up one end.

I know that the change has happened in my attitude—there has not been a sudden city-wide effort to make Jean feel comfortable.

Ah, how a few facts and a few days in a foreign country can make a difference.

You see, in New York City, I have always seen the people crunched in small apartments, using the stoops as meeting places and the street to wash or fix dilapidated cars as inherently "unhappy." I had an elitist attitude towards the inhabitants of the Dominican neighborhood surrounding my daughter's family's apartment. How could anyone who lives in a concrete, noisy jungle with no individual transportation be happy? In particular, I pitied the poor worker who had only a bicycle to get to work in NYC or in my home state of Oregon.

However, I read an article in a recent *New Yorker Magazine* that explored the roots of happiness. Two

research studies quoted continue to surprise me. For the first study, individuals who had either lost a leg or won the lottery were nearly back to their original biological set-point for happiness within a year of the event. Second, money directly correlated with happiness only under a very small minimum of $14,000 per year. Above that, happiness was more a matter of attitude than lack of basic survival resources. Only one factor under our individual control seems to consistently increase our happiness quotient: volunteering.

My other "aha" came from a short trip to Nicaragua. I visited at the invitation of a former student who was volunteering with JICA, the Japanese equivalent of the Peace Corps. Having lived in the country for two years and committed to live as the 'Nicas,' she knew how to travel cheaply and she took me with her into her world. As the twentieth passenger added to a fifteen passenger van, I had a first-hand experience in appreciating any kind of gasoline-powered means of getting from one place to another. And once, while in such a van, we passed a family of four on one bicycle, a prized and treasured possession.

I realized that the people I saw on the crowded streets of New York or the rural roads of Nicaragua had many things that are the bedrock of happiness apart from money: family, friends, stimulation, community. How shallow my former perspective seemed.

—*Jean Moule, Oregon. Photos: Nana Jean in New York (left); and with children in Nicaragua (above).*

Nana Jean in New Orleans: *Remnants of Hurricane Katrina*

In November 2008 I was in New Orleans for a conference and I visited the Ninth Ward, the area hardest hit by Hurricane Katrina. It was a startling experience, especially because I was able to speak to people who were directly impacted by the life-changing events.

As I drove, I wondered what the numbers and letters on the houses meant. Well, they indicated which agency had searched the house and when, as well as whether there were dogs and cats that needed feeding and how many dead people had been in the house.

As I crossed the bridge into the Ninth Ward, I drove slowly through the streets. I felt very much alone and isolated in the midst of those almost ghostly neighborhoods. Where were the sounds of children playing? I also saw closed and boarded-up schools.

The next day, I drove to the Ninth Ward with my sister and a friend. We parked next to an earth levee and walked to the top. From the top we saw downtown New Orleans and many boats along the river.

Our next stop was a "Green" house, built to maximize green technology and use little electricity and water. Some new homes are being built this way. When we turned the next corner, we saw a man, Royce, near his home. He talked about the neighborhood. He told us that the house across the street had just been demolished two weeks ago. He told us about his own struggles, how his insurance covered only the replacement of his wind-damaged roof. He did all the work of gutting the interior and reconstruction himself. He talked about his new sectional sofa and washer and dryer lost in the flood. Just ordinary things turned upside down, sometimes literally.

Continuing down the street, we came to an art gallery. I was touched by the water-damaged photographs on display. At the gallery we were encouraged to stop by the "Brad Pitt" and "Space-Age" houses (called the "Make it Right" project).

We drove by these new, brightly colored houses on Tennessee Avenue: houses on stilts, houses with solar panels. Among them was a granite memorial for two people who had died in Katrina: a three-year-old child and her great grandmother who both lost their lives near there in the wake of Katrina on August 29, 2005.

Another day I drove with other friends onto Tennessee Avenue. As we got out of the car, we saw a man in the distance at a playground with two kids. He waved at us. At the memorial, I read the names: Joyce and Shanai Green, ages 73 and 3. I have two three-year old grandchildren, so it really touched my heart.

As we were getting back into the car the man who had waved began walking toward us with two of his surviving grandchildren, Muffin and Shaniya (now 5 and 7), were dressed alike and seem happy and cordial.

As he approached I noticed his face was wet and there were tears in his eyes. He introduced himself. as Robert Green Jr., 54; Joyce Green was his mother and Shanai, his granddaughter.

Robert told us stories of how his family left the ward twice, and were told to return, how a barge hit the levee three blocks from his home, and caused a 20-foot wave to surge into his neighborhood sweeping his home off its foundation and moving it blocks away. He struggled to protect and save his family.

He and his brother managed to get their wheelchair-bound mother, a mentally disabled adult cousin, and the three grand babies into the attic before the home was swept away. It caught on another house and as Robert moved the children to the roof of the other, stable house, NaiNai and his mother fell off the roof into the water. He screamed, "Jesus!" He was able to rescue his mother and resuscitate her, but the child disappeared into the waters. An older grandchild fell in as well, but was able, at the age of 4, to swim to a truck roof where the whole family ended up, to await rescue. Sometime around 1 pm, Joyce died. But before she passed away, she said, "I'll take care of NaiNai."

When I shared this story with my students at Oregon State University, one student, who had returned from Iraq shortly after Katrina, said he was deployed to New Orleans for three weeks. He told of the chaos and the inadequate human resources. He said it was worse than the war zone.

This sad and personal story made me cry. It also helped me realize how much building and healing still needs to happen in the Ninth Ward of New Orleans.

Nana Jean Goes to Mount Kilimanjaro

Nana Jean decided to go to Tanzania, Africa and climb Mount Kilimanjaro. This is the first part of her journey.

Here were some of my concerns when I first thought of doing this trip: I am afraid of getting altitude sickness, getting ill, and not getting enough sleep. Will I be able to get the right foot gear (I wear size 12, narrow)? Is age 62 a good age to do this? On the other hand, I looked forward to: getting in great shape while there; getting to the top; seeing unusual wildlife and experiencing a part of Africa; and, when I am back, sharing my trip with others.

December 13: Well…two days to go and I am pacing the house—I am very nervous. Am I fit enough? What am I doing?! I needed some reassurance.

December 14: In the morning when I was at the dentist's office, I read the wall poster in the room:

Realize your dream from A to Z:

B. Believe in yourself
J. Just do it
L. Live life today. Yesterday is gone, tomorrow may..
M. Make it happen
T. Take control of your own destiny
V. Visualize it
W. Want it more than anything else

Later that day we did an exercise in my deep water aerobics class called "Climbing a Mountain."

So, finally, I feel assured that this is what I should do! Climb a mountain, climb Kilimanjaro.

I get ready by exercising in the water twice a week and going for a run at least once a week. I pack very lightly knowing that I will wear the same clothes for most of my six days on the mountain. I decide to wear my hiking boots and only take a carry-on bag. My trekking poles stick out of the top!

December 15: Leaving Portland, Ore. and the U.S.

My husband wakes me up around 7:20 AM. My flight out of Portland is a little late, but I make the flight out of Seattle on time. It takes forever to take off…de-icing, etc. During this flight to Amsterdam, I do not sleep at all. Instead, I watch three movies.

December 16: The layover at the Amsterdam Airport is just the right length (still can't believe my carry-ons are working out with the two trekking poles sticking out). There is a nice little museum there with Ruisdael paintings I enjoy.

Another nine-hour flight to Kenya. I enjoy flying over Europe *(who knows which countries)*, the Alps and then the Mediterranean Sea. What a huge sea! By the time we are over Africa, I am so tired I can't keep my eyes open. It is amazing to look down at the endless Sahara and the sparsely populated areas.

Finally, we land at the Kilimanjaro Airport in the dark. A man meets me at the gate with a sign with my name on it.

It's warm but too dark to see any landscape, and it is a long drive to my overnight stay at the Ngurdoto Lodge. I am very excited, but I sleep well.

Early the next morning I wake, eager, but almost scared. The landscape is beautiful. I pack and leave some things at the lodge, just taking my gear for climbing the mountain. The air is warm, and the birds and flowers are unusual to me. I enjoy talking to the people who are at the reception desk and even find a computer center so I can tell my family I have arrived safely and will not be able to contact them for six days.

Finally, I meet my guide, Max, and we drive an hour to Marangu gate where my adventure will begin. Once, we stop to take a photo of Kilimanjaro. Kili is quite unusual in that it is a free standing mountain, not connected to a range. It rises right out of the plains around it. Such a surprise to see snow on its peak in a very hot region of the world. When we arrive at the Marangu gate, I sign in, very solemnly. I find out later that at each stop, I will have to sign a ledger that says I have made it that far. Everyone who enters Kilimanjaro Park must have a guide, and every single person has three to eight people supporting them on the trek. Max finds a cook, a server and a porter to climb with us. Food for the climbers and the support team has to be carried up the mountain. I am so very excited to begin…

(To be continued in the next issue)

Nana Jean Goes to Mt. Kilimanjaro, Part II

Nana Jean went to Tanzania, Africa and climbed Mount Kilimanjaro. Here is the rest of her journey:

17 December: *Marangu Gate to Mandara Hut (6,000 to 9,000 feet).*

Every person who climbs Mt. Kilimanjaro must have a guide. My guide, Max, speaks excellent English, which is quite a plus for me.

When we get to Marangu Gate, we sign in and pay the fees. Then we begin to walk. I pass others and I get passed by others. I stop by a little waterfall pool in order to fill my water bottle using my filter. I know that hydration is the key to acclimating to high altitude. I had heard there are crowds of people on this trail, but where are they?

At this point there is a road that goes straight up: for porters and rescue vehicles only. Visitors and guides must use the trail. Now I begin to see more people, including some coming down. "It's exhausting," say the ones who are coming down from the top.

In the bunkhouse there are many beds in a row with four inch foam pads on the bunk. After I put my own pad on that, it is very comfortable. Meals include more courses than I can eat. Usually it is soup, bread, vegetables, starch, sauce (at times with meat) and fruit.

After dinner I weigh my bags: 16 pounds total. I may try to get it down a pound or two before tomorrow, as even that light weight is hurting my shoulders on the long hauls.

18 December: *Mandara to Horombo Hut (12,000 ft.).*

I am very slow today, taking about 7 and a half hours on a normal 5-7 hour trek to reach Horombo Huts at 12,000 feet. Max tells me stories of groups he has guided as we walk; he has guided people from all over the world up this mountain.

19 December: *Acclimate at Horombo Hut (12,000 feet).*

In the morning I walk up to Zebra Rocks at 13,020 ft., and back. At camp, I give Max and Reginald their choice of wrist watches as part of my planned tip.

Last night, after a hint from a fellow traveler, I filled my water bottle with hot water, a trick that certainly helped keep me warm.

View at Horombo Hut

20 December: *To Kibo Hut (15,570 ft).*

The landscape between Horombo and Kibo is mostly high desert. On the way up we get sleet and snow.

I sign in at reception when I arrive at Kibo. Instead of 3 or 4 person huts, I am in a ten person room, and because the huts are not heated, we all snuggle in our bags to stay warm. We will leave at midnight in order to make the top by sunrise.

21 December: *Summit (19,340 ft.) and down*

Max wakes me at 10:30 PM, and we are ready to climb the mountain by 11:14 PM. So many days, so many miles, and now the time has come.

We climb by the light of a three-quarter moon in silence to save lung capacity and air. Right before the Hans Meyers cave that sits at about 17,000 feet, I have to stop two times. That scares me because I know I will not make it if I stop that often. I also know that most attrition on the climb happens after the cave. Fortunately, a 10-minute rest is refreshing and I am able to continue on at a better pace.

Finally, when my GPS says 17,786 feet, I believe ***I Will Succeed!***

We reach Gilman's Point at 18,750 feet, a place where many stop their climb. After only a minute or two, Max urges me on towards the summit.

At this point, Max becomes terribly ill. He is bleeding from the nose. He later tells me that on a scale from 1 to 10, his headache is a 10, and he has never felt this bad in his life and must turn back. He tells me to go on, that I should look for his uncle Dismas, a guide I have met earlier, and tell him what has happened.

I struggle around the rocks to the crater rim. I am barely sure of where I might be and am very worried about Max, for I know he must be extremely ill to leave me on my own.

After a few minutes, I come up to the almost flat

trail around the crater. Many other routes to the top join in here and there is a big crowd. I am not even sure which way to go, but my GPS, set on the summit, shows an arrow and a distance of 0.57 miles. I proceed in that direction, following along with everyone else, looking in vain for someone I know.

Finally, I spot Dismas coming through the mist, and he continues the short distance to the summit, Uhuru Peak, with me. After taking a photo at the top, Dismas congratulates me again.

On the way down the mountain I begin to struggle. This day involves 4,000 feet up and 7,000 feet down, and the snow has made the descent slippery and treacherous. Finally, in an area of dirt and mixed snow, I stop and remember scree sliding. I give up on the poles and trust my muscle memory and balance from skiing. I make good time down a large portion of the slope to Kibo Hut, where I arrive only 30 minutes after Max, who has improved a little.

At this point, I fall exhausted into my bag. I am thinking, "Can I fake a medical emergency? Is the cloud cover high enough for a helicopter rescue?" But I am dragged out of bed by my crew. We, who are resting before continuing down, have to vacate so that those coming up to Kibo for the night have bunks.

22 December: *Horombo Hut to Marangu Gate*

We start down in fairly good weather, and Max's headache has subsided to a level 4, but he decides to take the rescue truck anyway, saving us the last two hours of walking. He later tells me this illness was a recurrence of malaria.

At the bottom, I receive my certificate, buy a map and postcards, give out tips. My gear is put together, and we begin the long drive to Ngurdoto Lodge.

Kilimanjaro makes its own weather. I've had rain, sleet, hail, snow and sun. Fortunately, I did not get soaked to the skin until the last leg back today. Never has a warm bath felt so good!!

23 December: *Safari*

Awoke several times during the night; my bed seemed hard. I went to breakfast at 6 AM, and I ate lei-surely while writing postcards.

Emmanuel is my driver today and will take me on safari into Tarangire National Park. As we drive on the Savannah in an open jeep, we see zebras, impalas, red-billed and horned-bill birds, elephants far away, elephants near by, elephants young and old. Then we see duikers, waterbucks, banded mongoose, ostriches, warthogs, giraffes, baboons, monkeys and lions.

Most Awe-inspiring: The baboons, especially the cute little infants clinging to their mothers. The baboons live among impalas. Apparently, the baboons will warn the impalas when predators come, but they will sometimes eat an impala infant themselves.

Most Surprising: At the picnic area I had just opened my lunch box when, in a blink of an eye, a velvet monkey grabbed my bread! Good thing she did not get my delicious chicken!

Most Unexpected: We see three lions. They're a rare sight in this park. I am very satisfied with the safari.

Most Unique: The gigantic and old Baobab trees.

We return through Masai country to Arusha. The houses are often made of mud and colored the same as the landscape. We drive through an open market where we see many men and women all clothed in bright blue and red garments. Along the road, many children herding goats wave at us as we drive past them. At one place, I stop to buy a bracelet for my granddaughter, Bella, from a women with a darling, one-month-old daughter. I wish I had more time or could have had my grandchildren with me.

24 December: *Christmas Eve. Home!*

I am ready for my long, long journey home.

I am dropped off at the Kilimanjaro Airport nine hours before my flight. Shopping, eating and sharing stories with other summiteers fill my time. After many hours in the air and two changes of planes I am home to my family.

I wonder, what next? Climb Mount Fuji in Japan? Learn to fly an airplane? Something high.

—*Prof. Jean Moule, Oregon State University, Oregon.*

Nana Jean: *What I learned about Grandparenting in China*

"I love that you are making the Chinese babies laugh! Laughter cuts across all language barriers!" said a friend while looking at this photo, and I thought how so many things cross cultures so naturally. For example, I find most babies and small children will laugh if I swing my hair. Then I stop, and there is a wonderful smile for a good photo; this is what happened at a temple in China we visited!

My husband, a.k.a. Pops or Popsie, enjoyed my connection with this child. He asked, "Did we enjoy our own children as much as we enjoy our grandchildren? And do other grandparents feel the same way?" He explained, the more transgenerational interactions he sees, the more he finds we, as grandparents, are not alone in feeling this way. Something happens between grandparents and their grandchildren that supplements what children are getting from their own parents. Whether grandparents are around because of financial difficulty, sickness, tradition or strong family ties, they have the ability to be positively involved in the development of their grandchildren, as well as receive love and emotional satisfaction from them in return.

Last July we had the opportunity to spend two weeks in China and were able to witness many examples of grandparents spending time with their grandchildren. In a country where most couples are only allowed to have one child, both parents and grandparents want the very best for their offspring. Many times families would encourage their children as young as eight or nine to approach us, ask how we were and welcome us to China. As children did this, in English, the parents and/or grandparents would be beaming with

pride. During the day when both parents were working, the children, including infants, would be cared for by their grandparents. This is exactly what my photo of the grandbaby with a caring grandpa exhibits.

With our family, we have enhanced our ability to spend time with our far-flung grandchildren by having a "Cousins Camp" every summer. Each year there is a theme, and we often choose it a year ahead. So far, some themes we have had are Bunnies, Frogs, and Dinosaurs. This year—Birds. While we were in China I tried to get as many bird-themed items as possible. I found cloisonné birds, birds in jade, calligraphy birds, embroidered birds, painted birds and a thoroughly annoying plastic parrot with a silly vocabulary.

Our program at our Cousins Camp this year included a live rooster, for that is both the shape and a symbol of China, as well as a play about birds interacting. The highlights though, were the contributions by two of the grandchildren who just happened to be studying China! Ainsley (6) and Bella (4) could both count in Chinese and tried to teach us grown ups. Bella sang an action song in Chinese, and we all joined in with the actions, though not the words.

Our memories of China and Chinese families were enhanced as we worked with our own grandchildren this summer. Our theme next year? Insects! And I already have some bugs embedded in plastic that I have picked up in China.

Book Recommendation:

The Hello, Goodbye Window *by Norton Juster and Chris Raschka (Hyperion). It includes a Nanna and Poppy that look like Nana and Popsie, and they also have a similar house.*

Nana Jean Goes to Hawai'i: *The 50th State in the Union*

Hawaii became a state in 1959. I was fortunate as a child and young adult to visit every other state in the Union, including Alaska (the other distant state which also joined the Union earlier in 1959). Somehow, for me the islands of Hawaii remained distant, unapproachable, set in the middle of the Pacific Ocean. Finally, about 8 years ago, I visited Hawaii for the first time to attend a wedding. Since then, I have gone to visit the Big Island four times, Kauai once, and this time, the island of Maui. Interested in both archeology and culture, I'd like to share my reflections on the clash of cultures that I have seen on these trips. Hawaii is indeed a paradise, one with a tension based in cultural differences.

Consider a few questions, for example:

What if the most important thing in your life is family? What if the most important thing in your life is nature? What if the most important thing in your life is some thing else? (You can write it here _____).

What happens when you meet and get to know someone whose "most important thing" is much different than yours?

We just came back from Maui, Hawaii, and thought about how different the feelings and "most important things" were to the people living there.

Those who have been there "longest" have generations of family going back hundreds of years. We saw large extended families gathered on beaches on weekends (and even other times) for joint meals and community time. Their ancestors had come to the island over thousands of miles of sea, following the stars and currents. They have established a culture and a connection to this warm and fertile land that is deep, lasting... and very spiritual.

Those who have relocated to Hawaii in recent years find themselves thousands of miles away from their families. They love the beauty and the warmth of the islands. They may have important goals of enjoying a lifestyle that includes material possessions and, per-

haps, the means to get back to the families they left behind. Yes, it brings money and jobs to the island, and there is a 13% tourist tax in Hawaii that supports government services.

And many people from the mainland travel to enjoy the beauty and wonder of the islands for a very short time. They stay in places by the beach to swim and sit in the sun. Hawaiians use the beaches differently: big family BBQs, fishing and memorials to those family members who have died.

What happens when these "most important" things meet in a place like Hawaii?

What happens when a large resort takes over a beach that was your family's sacred space and place to gather?

While the Hawaiian law says that **all beaches should have public access**, including trails to the beaches, there are often little or no parking spaces nearby and the access routes are difficult to find. Sometimes, the resorts make discouraging barriers for beach access.

We found that we enjoyed the beaches with easy access and with native people on them, however, we could also see why some beaches seemed set aside for some specific purposes or groups like kiteboarders or windsurfers. Some beaches were natural draws to surfers and snorkelers because of the way the ocean and shore meet.

When people from different cultural backgrounds meet, they have a choice to make: do we make assumptions about our right to impose our own way of knowing and being? Or, are we respectful and open? Certainly in Hawaii, there is much to gain from looking at the ways the Hawaiians have interacted with the natural world and the creatures in it.

As I left the islands I was reminded of my need to be open and caring with those I meet, particularly those whose culture is different than mine. I hope you will do the same in your interactions.

Nana Jean says *Aloha*

"You can't really understand Barack until you understand Hawai'i."
—*First Lady Michelle Obama*

*P*resident Obama is a kama'āina, or land child, born in Hawai'i. Are there specifics in Hawai'i's culture and history that help him to be a good president? As kama'āina Obama was raised and went to school among people from different places and cultures that learned to live in harmony.

Aloha: a common greeting. It means *more* than '*Hello.*' That *more* may help us to understand the deep roots of our president's outlook that may serve our diverse nation well. It was in Hawai'i that he came to believe "that our patchwork heritage is a strength, not a weakness." Obama speaks specifically of his family: "As a child of a black man and a white woman, someone who was born in the racial melting pot of Hawai'i, with a sister who's half Indonesian…and a brother-in-law and niece of Chinese descent…I've never had the option of restricting my loyalties on the basis of race, or measuring my worth on the basis of tribe."

Aloha means giving from the heart in a respectful manner. It means mutual regard and affection, and extends warmth in caring with no obligation in return. Each person is important to all others for collective existence. Obama said, "That's why we pass on the values of empathy and kindness to our children by living them."

In the concepts below, based on the Hawai'ian language, I've included quotes from Obama to help us understand how the concepts have impacted him.

Mana: divine spirit or power that is in every person, rock and flower. Today people of all faiths live in Hawai'i side by side. Hawai'ians practice many faiths: Christian, Jewish, Muslim, Hindu or Buddhist. Obama says, "faith is not just something you have, it is something you do."

'Aina: the land. "Growing up in Hawai'i, not only do you appreciate the natural beauty, but there is an ethic of concern for the land that dates back to native Hawai'ians."

Akahai: kindness.

'Olu'olu: agreeable. "No place else could have provided me with the environment, the climate, in which I could not only grow, but also get the sense of being loved."

Akamai: smart, clever, skilled, expert. "There is so much out there that you can be curious about and learn about." Obama says that his school "embraced me, gave me support, gave me encouragement and allowed me to grow and to prosper."

Kuleana: privilege, duty and responsibility. "Individual responsibility and mutual responsibility—that's the essence of America's promise."

Ahonui: patience, perseverance. "I want us to think about the long term and not just the short term."

Kōkua: help, aid, assist, support, helping to get something done. "If we see somebody who's in need, we should help."

Kupuna: ancestor, grandparent, respected elder. Obama explains how his grandmother took care of him and taught him so much, and her importance in his life.

Keiki: child. Everyone older is called Auntie or Uncle when you are small. And keiki are cherished by all. "These children are our children. Their future is our future."

'Ohana: family. "The essence of Hawai'i has always been that we come from far and wide, that we come from different backgrounds and different faiths, and different last names, and yet we come together as a single 'ohana because we believe in the fundamental commonality of people…Of all the rocks upon which we build our lives, we are reminded today that family is the most important."

Lōkahi: unity, harmony, agreement, creating unity. "It must be about what we can do together."

Mahalo: respect and thank you.

Ha'aha'a: humililty, modesty. "We look out for one another…we deal with each other with courtesy and respect. And most importantly, when you come from Hawai'i, you start understanding that what's on the surface, what people look like, doesn't determine who they are."

Pono: fair, just and good.

Ho'oponopono: working things out, resolving conflict, talking, listening, forgiving. "What people often note as my even temperament I think draws from Hawai'i… there just is a cultural bias toward courtesy and trying to work through problems in a way that makes everybody feel like they're being listened to."

"People ask me, they say, 'What do you still bring from Hawai'i?'…I try to explain to them something about the aloha spirit… And it's that spirit that I am absolutely convinced is what America is looking for right now."

Most of the quotes above come from the book, **"A President from Hawai'i"** *(Banana Patch Press, 2009). It was one of three books that enlightened my third trip to Maui and my eighth trip to Hawai'i.*

Nana Jean *on European Customs*

How do young children process culture when they travel and experience different languages, customs and clothing? I went with my family, including two of my grandchildren *(Photo: Jamie, 7, and Ainsley, 9)* for a week of travels in Italy. We skied in high mountains and walked among thousands in Venice.

Ainsley said, "In France and Spain, I could speak with the native people who live there. But Italians speak Italian, and I have not learned to speak Italian." She added, "It was a strange experience for me."

During our six days in Italy we did not see another family from the United States while we were skiing. We were very grateful that most of the people around us spoke English and were often eager to speak it with us. We found out that the children in the local school are first taught Italian, then Ladin, a regional language, and then English, beginning at age 7.

The differences in clothing had a strong impact on us. In Venice we watched a woman from a Middle Eastern culture go by in a gondola. Her hair and face were covered except for her eyes. It was strange for me and my grandchildren. They also noticed a difference when we went to the sauna in our "pension" in Corvara, Italy. "I cannot believe that the Europeans go in saunas naked!" Ainsley said. She was used to the custom in the United States of people entering saunas, hot tubs and steam rooms in public places wearing their bathing suits. We talked at length about the differing custom. While I encouraged my grandchildren to wear bathing suits so they were comfortable, as is accepted in our culture in the United States, I also questioned their response to the more natural custom they saw in Italy. Is it "disgusting" and "gross"? No. It is just different. Respect for others' cultural differences starts with this simple understanding: differences do not mean "less than," especially when traveling.

Another simple custom difference we found was how to get in and out of our rooms. In the United States, hotels usually give you a card key or a metal key for your room. In Europe, and many other places around the world, you almost always leave your room keys at the main desk when you are not in the hotel. It is usually attached to a large piece of leather or wood: too bulky to easily fit in your pocket. This custom allows the hotel to know when you are in your room or not. It also means you are less likely to take the key with you! It took us a few days to learn to automatically leave our key on the hook near the front desk.

In Italy, we noticed that there was more crowding to get into places and longer lines for ski lifts. Yet in the United Kingdom, we experienced very clear "queues," or orderly lines for getting on buses and into other places. I believe some of these customs may vary quite a bit depending on regions within any country. At times, in the Dolomites of Italy, we found that if we were too polite and waited as we do in the U.S., it was a while before we got into a ski gondola or tram!

Then there was the process of getting service in places to eat. In Italy, I found I did not even know the simple way to get food in restaurants or "refugios," on the mountains where we skied. Sometimes we ordered inside and the food was brought out. Other times we ordered at the tables. Because I do not know Italian, I had a difficult time finding out which to expect! Also, do you pay when you order? Or, do you pay when you are finished? Do you take your dishes to a collection station or leave them on your table? These simple understandings are "scripts," often unspoken interactions that we come to know within our own culture or community, yet have difficulty understanding elsewhere. The children also noticed differences in the meals. Ainsley noted that "everybody eats much later than in the U.S." and "It's four course meals!"

These differences have helped me pay more attention and be more adaptable. In our global world and our increasingly diverse classrooms, this is a skill we all need to practice.

Aim High

Faith of all kinds help us to see ourselves and our worlds in the light of daring, caring, risking, dreaming and expecting more than what seems possible, practical or wise at first. May you aim high as you choose/try/decide to make a difference.

Nana Jean: Facing Challenges

" *75765, is there an instructor on board?"* My erratic taxiing had been noted by the control tower.

The basics of flying seemed so difficult. Maybe it was a good thing that the threatening weather kept my instructor and me on the ground in our plane. I stared through the raindrops on the aircraft windshield. Would I ever learn to fly?

I have seen my grandchildren and my students begin a difficult task, become frustrated and put the material or task down with a sigh, lacking the will to continue. I have learned how to help them move past the barriers and try again. Could I do that for myself?

Rarely in my adult life have I faced tasks I found challenging beyond learning a new skill on the computer or how to work a new appliance or gadget. And rarely do these tasks have high emotional impact or the kinds of pressure one may experience when the task is complex, cognitively difficult and watched over intently by a teacher.

Perhaps I needed a reminder of such experiences. Five years ago in "Ask Nana Jean," I wrote about my climb up Mount Kilimanjaro in Tanzania and concluded with my desire to reach more heights. Climb another mountain? Learn to fly? And that is how I found myself behind the controls of an airplane, in the pilot's seat with the instructor on the controls on my right. Could I reach high places in a plane?

This was my third lesson; this time with a substitute instructor. The checklist with 120 items and a cockpit with a lot more dials than a car seemed bewildering. Afterwards, as I paid for my half hour on the ground my head filled over and over with "Why am I doing this?" I reminded myself: I want to learn to fly:

- Because I like heights
- Because I want additional perspectives
- Because I need exhilaration and a new challenge

I drove home feeling dejected, the rain and gray clouds matching my mood. I knew that at some point I would have to find the reserves to try again. I tried to encourage myself by thinking about other challenging things I have accomplished:

- Learning to drive a car
- Handling an excavator
- Learning to ski or pull a sled while on ski patrol
- Learning to teach!

I made a list of resolutions and requests that I believed would help me continue on:

- Get a copy of the preflight checklist and go over it at home
- Get a life-sized poster of the cockpit and practice touching the right switches
- Ask my instructor to taxi next time to at least get us off the ground

And finally, I remembered the pleasure I receive when my own students begin to grasp a concept that is hard for them. So my final reason for continuing with my lessons? My instructors may feel blessed when their challenging and challenged student finally makes progress. They, too, will have a student whose success they will remember fondly…when she finally learns to fly solo.

Ten days later, my journal entry read:

"I flew today. My instructor watched as I turned the plane over our house, circled the small town of Lyons where we used to live, and flew over the road I take to work. Up and down. Level flight, smooth turns and a deep satisfaction. Now, I need to learn to take off and land!

"What a contrast to just a few days ago when I almost put down my pilot log-book for good."

My words for myself and others: when the journey gets tough, be strong and continue on. No matter how long it takes.

Nana Jean: *Bessie Coleman*

Who was the first American to hold an international pilot license?

As a challenge, I decided that I wanted to learn to fly a small airplane. My flight instructor knew I needed to learn about other Black women who had flown. First, he connected me to a Black female student pilot. Then he introduced me to the legendary Bessie Coleman.

Bessie was born in Texas in 1892 as one of 13 children of a couple who worked in the cotton fields. She was good at math, loved books and walked eight miles round trip to attend a one-room school for Blacks. She went to Oklahoma where she studied for one term at a university, but had to leave due to lack of money.

In 1915, at age 23, Bessie moved to Chicago. She lived with her brothers and worked as a fingernail manicurist in the city. In Chicago, she heard and read stories of World War I soldiers and pilots as they returned from Europe. She and her brother, a soldier, talked.

"Those French women do something no Colored girl has done," her brother teased. "They fly."

Taking that as a challenge, Bessie decided to become a pilot. Due to both race and gender discrimination, she gave up trying to enter a flight school in the United States and began her study of French. She learned the language well enough to grasp the principles of flight and the technical aeronautic terms in that language. Then she went to France to learn to fly.

She completed a ten-month course in just seven months to receive her pilot's license. She returned to the U. S. to fly. She wanted to start flight schools for African Americans. She earned her living barnstorming and performing aerial tricks, specializing in stunt flying and parachuting.

Bessie's high-flying skills wowed audiences of thousands. She was well known all over the United States, making big headlines whenever she flew in air shows.

During a rehearsal for an air show in 1926, she leaned out of an airplane flown by her mechanic to check her planned parachute-landing site. The plane began an unexpected tailspin towards the ground.

Bessie, who was unbelted at the time, was thrown out of the plane and fell 1,500 feet to her death.

Afterwards others took up her cause to begin flight schools that allowed Blacks' entry. Some of those inspired by her daring learned to fly in these schools and were early enrollees in the World War II Black Tuskegee Airmen Division. I found out that my grandson's great-grandfather was a flight instructor for those airmen!

Bessie's legacy continued on through the years. In 1929, the aviation school she worked to establish was founded in Los Angeles. Roads, highways and flying clubs for women were named after her. In 1995, the U.S. Postal Service issued a Bessie Coleman stamp. And every year on Memorial Day, the Tuskegee Airmen fly over Brave Bessie's grave and drop flowers in her honor.

Bessie Coleman once said, "Do you know that you have never lived until you have flown?" While few fly in small airplanes, many people have been able to fly in large jets. My children have all flown commercially, as have my grandchildren. One grandchild, Chance, the great grandson of Tuskegee Airman instructor, James A. Hill, leads the rest: before he was five years old he had flown on 120 flight segments.

For leading the way, I give my thanks to Elizabeth "Bessie" Coleman, the first American aviator of any race or gender to hold a license to fly anywhere in the world, the first African American to be licensed in the U. S., and a pioneer in aviation education for all people.

—Professor Jean Moule, Oregon, with grandson Chance.

Ask Nana Jean *about Role Models like Yourself*

First Lady Michelle Obama was the commencement speaker at Oregon State University (OSU) on June 17, 2012. I wrote this letter to her.

Dear Michelle,

As far as I know, you are the second woman of African descent to speak at an OSU commencement: I was the speaker for the 2003 graduate ceremony. At that time the graduations were separated: the undergraduates had a "guest" speaker and the graduate students had a faculty member. I was both honored and humbled to be chosen to give a 12-minute address that June day to the Masters and Doctoral candidates.

I plan to be in the audience on the 17th as a faculty representative and I look forward to it all: the excitement, the security, and the incredible opportunity to listen to a female speaker who reflects my hue. This is simply beyond my wildest expectations. As an activist and one who has been part of the struggle, your presence speaks of much progress.

Thank you for coming. I do hope the day goes very well for you.

I am emeritus now in the College of Education. This event will be the last time I will wear my academic regalia, passing it on to my lawyer daughter who will wear it in her duties as a college trustee at Voorhees College.

I thought you might like to read the speech I gave.

The best to you, First Lady Michelle.

Professor Jean Moule

I received a gracious form letter reply from the White House. While I doubt the First Lady ever read my speech, I have a warmer spot in my heart for her speech because I tried to share mine. I was seated in the first row, but I could see her much better on the large screens. I was struck by her humility and enthusiasm. Her speech addressed neither the presidential politics nor race relations!

Of the many things she shared with the graduates and their families and friends, one theme struck home for me: What is a measure of success? First of all, she said, "The true measure of your success is… not how well you do when you're healthy, and happy and everything is going according to plan. But what you do when life knocks you to the ground and all your plans go right out the window. In those darkest moments, you have a choice: Do you dwell on everything you've lost? Or do you focus on what you still have, and find a way to move forward with passion, and determination, and joy?"

Mrs. Obama further defined the importance of passion over money for career choice. She told us the story of her (and her brother's) struggles to succeed in school, through college and in their early careers. "We soon had all the traditional markers of success—the fat paycheck, the fancy office, the impressive line on our resumes. But the truth is, neither of us was all that fulfilled. I didn't want to be up in some tall office building writing legal memos; I wanted to be down on the ground, helping the folks I grew up with. I was living the dream—but it wasn't my dream." By the world's and by money's standards, they were both "highly successful." Yet their jobs in finance and law were not inspiring. Each choose to take less money for more personal satisfaction. They redefined success for themselves. And in that choice rose spectacularly in their new fields of coaching and service.

The most emotional moment for me came when the graduating students, who were also in one of the campus military officer training units, were commissioned. Before the First Lady, they took an oath of office with their hands over their hearts. As they finished, two military jets flew over. It was a thrilling sight!

Mrs. Obama left after the degrees were conferred and while graduates were lining up to receive their individual diplomas. It was a last event for me as a faculty member on the field in my gown. It was a first for me to see the wife of the highest official in the land surrounded by pomp, circumstance and high security, walking in her brown skin and regal bearing to give inspiration and encouragement to us all.

The other day while my seventh grade class watched a movie, I made myself up like Nefertiti and then dramatically read the story of the opening of King Tut's tomb and the faith of the Egyptians in the afterlife. I told the class there would be a special guest today. The teacher's book says that this period in Egyptian history is contemporaneous with the Hebrews and that the Bible may be used as a reference. *What if I dress like Moses?*

Where is the line between teaching about religion and practicing religion in the classroom? Wouldn't it be easier, as the beginning teachers in my college classes suggest, to just keep religion out of the classroom completely? Children representing many faiths and no faith, including agnostics or atheists, attend public schools in most nations. As our demographic and immigration patterns change we know that all children need to feel safe and included when it comes to religion or no religion. How do teachers remain wholesomely neutral in their classrooms? What are students allowed to say or do in regards to their faith?

Religion inspires "faith and morality for many people. Mosques, synagogues, sweat lodges, churches, temples, sacred mountains, ashrams, and cathedrals have been uplifting places of spiritual reflection and prayerful worship for human beings throughout recorded history…. No matter how religion and spirituality are understood, they are powerful forces in the lives of individuals—including teachers and students in schools." *(Patrick Slattery, 2006, p. 71).*

Each time we're confronted with an issue around religion in public schools, five factors come into play: legal issues, curriculum issues, moral issues, personal faith, and common sense. We will touch legal issues in another issue.

Many curriculum units help teachers teach about religion in an appropriate manner. Some guidance on curriculum issues may come directly from teachers' manuals. Two brochures, **Religion in the Public School Curriculum** and **Religious Holidays in the Public Schools** *(from Freedom Forum)* sponsored jointly by nine secular organizations, such as the NEA and AFT and seven religious organizations, like the National Council of Christians *and* American Jewish Congress, may serve as a beginning point for understanding many curriculum issues. The brochures are in *Question-and-Answer* format and are based on the assumption that in our society public schools are places for persons of all faiths or none. Schools and school teachers may neither uphold nor put down any religion. The brochures also make it clear that "education without appropriate attention to major religious influences and themes is incomplete education."

Moral issues means thinking about what "is the right thing to do" and is closely connected with the teaching of values. One of the brochures says, "Basic moral values that are recognized by the population at large (e.g., honesty, integrity, justice, compassion)" may be taught through discussion or by example without using religion to enforce them. At the same time "public schools may teach about the various religious and non-religious perspectives concerning the many complex moral issues confronting society, but such perspectives must be presented without adopting, sponsoring, or denigrating one view against another" *(brochure)*. The most important point is understanding that First Amendment neutrality doesn't mean being neutral on values or acting on those values for the good of children.

Personal faith issues are harder to clarify. Teachers need to find the balance between caring for students and not trying to get students to follow the teacher's own faith. As an example, I was asked to be involved with a memorial service for a child of parents who did not believe in God. It was a challenge because, as a teacher, I could not push my faith, yet, as a Christian, I wanted to share hope for heaven. As I prepared for this event, I found material the student had written that supported his faith (and mine), and I was able to share using his words. Students are always allowed to share their faith when the choice of topic is up to them in the classroom or when they are on their own time, for example, during lunch or recess or before and after school.

Common sense may prevail when a clear choice is not obvious. For instance, what if a student initiates a prayer with a teacher? Where is the line between promoting and denying the faith of the student? In one situation, where I knew the child and his family (and their faith tradition), I did pray with the student during school hours. Using common sense I prayed with the student in a semi-private manner on the side of the playground, confident that my actions were congruent with the parents' and student's belief system. I was not taking attention or time away from other students and felt that the needs of this student were compelling.

Back to Moses. I told the students I would go to the office to check and asked them to welcome our guest if I missed him in the hallway. I quickly made my way to the teachers' lounge, changed into a long, colorful robe, flowing white beard and sandals and returned. I knocked and majestically entered the room… as Moses, complete with the *Ten Commandments.* After the initial shock and one student's comment, *"Gee Moses, you sure got a tan wandering around in the desert,"* we discussed the connections and mutual influences of the Hebrew and Egyptian cultures, appropriately learning about religion.

Nana Jean: *Teaching Faith in the Public Schools*

As a kindergarten teacher, I was concerned that my kids learn good behavior. I chose some sayings from many sources, including the Biblical book of Proverbs that help children make good choices and learn simple character qualities. I made up hand motions to help the children learn the words. The quotes said things like, "Be kind to each other" and "A wise child thinks before speaking."

I posted the quotes on a classroom bulletin board, and I would ask the children to recite them as part of getting ready to read. A parent who was picking up a child after school, noticed some quotes had the source of Proverbs written below them. She questioned whether they were appropriate in a public school setting because they were from the Bible.

First, what were the curriculum issues? In the Kindergarten class, the "Wall of Inspiration" content was teacher-directed, with several curriculum focuses: public recitation, group camaraderie, reading readiness and classroom management. This "Wall of Inspiration" helps the children who read them to see a deeper purpose for school.

However, for the kindergarten class, if I taught again, I would select the quotes more carefully and search more actively for good advice from many traditions both secular and religious; I might ask the parents and students for suggestions. I would try to ensure that the quotes would not offend any child, and mirrored both the neighborhood and our larger, diverse society. Students have freedom to write about religion, for instance a grade school child is free to respond to an assignment, "What I will do during the winter break" with a religious theme.

I have also had a wall of quotes in the hallway of my building on our college campus. Here, college students were free to post any guiding quote they wished. They were free to post a religious quote. Bible verses and Native American prayers generally account for about 20% of the quotes on the wall. In the college classroom, I was able to encourage thinking about deeper matters in a wholesomely neutral manner. When I view the quotes in the hallway, I see a multiplicity of viewpoints and choices that encourages me as an individual in my quest to make my classes at any level safe for all students.

However, the kindergarten classroom, with teacher-selected quotes, is a different matter. The teacher, as an instrument of the State, must remain "wholesomely neutral" in religious matters. In retrospect, I believe I could have done a better job of balancing the sources for my "good advice" for young people, even though appropriate quotes from a religious source is legal.

Whatever our persuasion in religious matters, we have developed personal belief systems that help build our principles. Out of these principles come common values such as honesty, integrity, justice and compassion. In the interest of integrity and balance we need to incorporate strategies that do not ask us to ignore or abandon these values or the spiritual side of ourselves.

In 1998, President Clinton said, "Schools do more than train children's minds. They also help to nurture their souls by reinforcing the values they learn at home and in their communities. I believe that one of the best ways we can help out schools to do this is by supporting students' rights to voluntarily practice their religious beliefs, including prayer in schools.... For more than 200 years, the First Amendment has protected our religious freedom and allowed many faiths to flourish in our homes, in our work place and in our schools. Clearly understood and sensibly applied, it works." *(US Dept. of Education).*

In 1998, the U.S. Secretary of Education went on to include great detail about our responsibilities as agents of the state in regards to religion: "The United States remains the most successful experiment in religious freedom that the world has ever known because the First Amendment uniquely balances freedom of private religious belief and expression with freedom from state-imposed religious expression. Public schools can neither foster religion nor preclude it. Our public schools must treat religion with fairness and respect and vigorously protect religious expression."

Public schools may not provide religious instruction, but they may teach about religion, including the Bible or other scriptures, the history of religion, com-

"Children may make religious choices in public schools."

parative religion, and the role of religion in the history of the U. S. (and other countries), all of which are permissible public schools subjects. Similarly, to consider religious influences on art, music, literature and social studies are also allowed. Although public schools may teach *about* religious holidays, as well as their religious aspects and may celebrate the secular aspects of holidays, schools may not observe holidays as religious events or promote such observance by students.

The First Amendment, "Congress shall make no law respecting an establishment of religion, or prohibiting the free exercise thereof," and the wealth of case laws gives us some very specific guidance on legal issues. The Supreme Court held that reading the Bible for religious purposes and reciting the Lord's prayer in public schools during normal hours were unconstitutional as part of the assigned classwork. The same decision held that schools could teach about the history of religion, or religious art and music, or teach the Bible as literature in appropriate classes. Because public school teachers are employed by the State and speak for the State, they must be careful not to include religious messages in their classroom expression. But they should also respect the free exercise rights of students to include religious expression where appropriate. Teaching about religion in a non-coercive manner that does not advance or inhibit religious beliefs is both constitutionally protected and important in our society.

The eighth graders that I teach were learning about the early colonial period of American history, including the arrival of the Pilgrims. I dressed as a pilgrim and set up a one-room meeting house with the men on one side and the women on the other. It was around Thanksgiving, and I led a reading of a Psalm of Thanksgiving from the Bible. Immediately, a problem arose. In the spirit of loud praise the class became way too noisy with their simulated worship and I wondered how to quiet them. I began to have some misgivings. At this point, my disciplining could be seen as negating their obvious enthusiasm for this religious reenactment. Also, as I see it now, I crossed a legal line. Instead of simply teaching about religion I was asking them to participate in a worship service, and that would violate the law.

From a curriculum perspective, the lesson was successful in conveying the importance of faith to the new immigrants to the North American continent.

It would have met legal guidelines, I believe, if I had asked for volunteers and simply acted it out with a few students with the rest observing and discussing various issues. This would have been more consistent with my moral decision to offer students choices in such matters in order to honor their religious expressions.

As for personal faith issues, at first I truly enjoyed the turn of events, because I did feel as if I were worshipping. However, this very feeling helped me to recognize that I was crossing the line into practicing religion rather than teaching about religion. Finally, as for common sense, I could have more carefully anticipated that events such as these might occur.

As you may imagine, by now I had lost some confidence, and I was wondering how to bring the class to a successful close. At this point in time, one student, without telling me why, asked if he could talk to the class. I glanced at the clock, and noted that it was one minute until the bell rang, but I nodded to him, not sure how I was going to conclude this class period anyway.

He stood at the podium and with a passionate voice, spoke of his faith and urged others to join him in it. My mouth dropped open as the bell rang and students filed out.

Of course, this unexpected turn of events had no curriculum focus. As for legal issues, I had given up my place as the instructional leader and allowed a student to proselytize: this was clearly a violation of the Establishment Clause. Morally, I was not comfortable about the captive nature of the audience, and of common sense…there was none! The message happened to be consistent with my personal faith, but that is beside the point.

There are times when this student's speech may have been legal with an appropriate curriculum focus. For example, if the student was assigned to give a persuasive speech as part of a language arts class, and he had his choice of topics, he could have used his religious convictions as a basis of his speech. His talk would then have been one of many similarly persuasive speeches, as well as it would have met the course learning objectives. He also would have his own Free Exercise right to express his faith in his speech.

And, the most important point is to understand that First Amendment neutrality doesn't mean one must be neutral on values or acting on values for the good of children.

Nana Jean In Jamaica

I have had the pleasure of visiting schools in England, China, Ghana, Nicaragua, Trinidad and Jamaica. Sometimes I have been an observer, other times I have given materials, and once I even substituted for a missing teacher.

One particular experience taught me, in a new way, the value of an excellent teacher. With few resources, but with a keen understanding of her craft and her students this individual was amazing. I want to introduce Miss Hazel, a teacher at the St. Ann's Bay Primary School in Jamaica.

St. Ann's is really two schools in one: one from 7 AM to noon, and the other from 12:15 PM to 5 PM. Miss Hazel has taught the first grade for 36 years. I figured she must be a master teacher, and she is. Many of her strengths and techniques are largely invisible to casual observers. However, anyone who can engage over 30 first graders in active learning with no assistants and very little visible classroom management is, indeed, a master teacher.

Miss Hazel was very careful to set the stage for behavior during the lesson. She made sure she had every eye on her and all hands in laps. Anytime a child opened a book, or moved about, she was on it right away.

The day I visited, Miss Hazel had the students identify the letter "s" and make its sound. She wrote the main idea of the lesson on the board: "The letter 's' goes at the end of a 'doing word.'" She then had the children repeat at least twice: "At the end of the lesson *every* child will be able to add an 's' to a 'doing word.'"

From there she had them list "doing words." She had the children help her spell the words and she had *all* of the children act out each word, such as run, clean and eat, thus incorporating some lesson-related physical activity. Next, she had them close their eyes while she added an "s" to each word. Then they used a little rhythm to read the words: tap, tap, tap, clap, clap, clap, I see a word and it is _____. Then she had the children name the words she erased one by one while their eyes were closed (and teases them about peeking).

Next, she had them construct a sentence. She pointed to a child on a poster, whom they named Lisa; she had them help her spell the name on the board. Now the children are asked to come up with synonyms for "Lisa." They list: him, her, she, my cousin, mother, sister, etc. She talked them through all those, asking who agreed or disagreed and why. She even discussed what a "cousin" is. She was not harsh with those who were incorrect and respected their answers.

As sentences were constructed jointly on the chalkboard, she had a child act out "runs fast" and "runs slowly." My guess is that she chose "runs" out of all the "doing words" because it had worked well for her as an illustration in other years.

At this point she had all the boys and all the girls huddle by gender and come up with a sentence. She asked a member from each group to tell their sentences (they do not all agree on what was decided). The boys got, "Lisa can run." She chided them that they did not use the word she gave them, "runs." The girls had, "Mother runs faster than Father."

Next she had them make sentences in pairs. She asked for one person from each pair to share what they came up with. I did see her reorganize a couple of pairs, like one where a girl turned around to work with the girl behind her rather than the boy beside her. Miss Hazel also reminded a group of four girls that they were to be in groups of two.

As each pair shared their sentences, she clapped if they were correct, or folded her hands across her chest if the sentence was incorrect. Next, she had two children come to write their sentences on the board. The one who had spoken it aloud could come to the board to help, but not write. Finally, she had them take out meager workbooks.

A couple notes about the value of this observation for potential teachers visiting from the U.S.:

First, the visiting college students experience much from their unfamiliar living situations. They learn what to eat or not to eat what they are served. They sleep in a large room together and bond with people they would not otherwise have gotten to know. They learn to walk a distance to and from the schools—up a steep hill coming home in a hot climate.

At the schools they see teachers, such as Miss Hazel, teach well with few supplies and noise coming in over the low partitions. Once back home they might think: if Miss Hazel could do x then I can do y. If teachers could teach and if students learn in those conditions, what more can I do with so many resources?

—Dr. Jean Moule, Oregon.

Nana Jean: Let's Make a Difference in Our World

As a guide on the side, I ask my students to select a guiding quote: something that means a lot to them, something they read in a book, something they heard from a famous person or even a relative. I often borrow these quotes from my students and put them where they can help me! The one by my phone reminds me, *"The first step to wisdom is silence; the second is listening."* The quote on my computer gets me through writer's block: *"I can do all things through Him who strengthens me."* And the quote over my desk quiets my frustrations with: *"You may not be able to change the world, but at least you can embarrass the guilty."*

Our quote for now is, *"A genius is someone who aims for something that no one else can see…and hits it."* I would like you to find a use for this quote. Take a moment to put in another word for "genius" if you like. You could insert "innovator" or "risk-taker" or "one who makes a difference" or "going-to-get-this-done hard worker" if you wish.

Often, I close my eyes and think about whether or not to aim for something very difficult or out of reach. Sometimes it works out, sometimes not. When it does, I am encouraged to aim a bit higher and a little farther.

I recall a time that I aimed high, reaching for a mark that my teacher could not see. I disliked the way history was taught with monocultural perspectives, and I had to repeat a U.S. History class in summer school. I put my heart into it this time and wrote a stirring, creative beginning to my paper on the Oregon Trail. My teacher did not believe me, an African American student, when I told her I wrote it myself. Discouraged by her low expectations of minority students, I did not bother finishing the research paper and received another low grade. Her harshness and her assumptions hampered my interest in writing as well as in history.

Much later, as a classroom teacher, I found Oregon history peculiarly intriguing: Oregon hosted on its soil a moment of inclusion when York, a Black man who was Clark's slave, and Sacajawea, a Native woman, voted along with the rest of the Lewis & Clark Expedition for the location of its winter camp. Yet, Oregon's history is marred by racist laws. One law assessed blacks, Chinese and Hawaiians an annual $5 tax for the privilege of living in Oregon! This legacy of exclusion is seen today in the absence of people of color in many Oregon communities.

Reaching higher can be as simple as not telling or reacting to racist jokes. A quote from one of my students: *"I will never tell a racist joke, so I'm not racist, but… I have laughed at other people's racist jokes,"* and later in the course, *"It will never again be okay to laugh at a racist joke or even to keep silent when one is being told."* These students are beginning to understand their own roles in the subtle, often-hidden racism that surrounds us all. Every term, my students report to me that when they take the time to open their eyes, they notice that while shopping, driving or meeting, people of color are treated differently. One said, *"Race shouldn't matter, but in this country, it still does—to everybody."*

On a more complex level, let's consider my own case. I am one of very few African American faculty members at Oregon State University. What is it like to be this brown face in a sea of whiteness?

"It is as if we are all on a river that flows quietly and gently along. Most of my friends, students, and colleagues float on this river in a strong, sturdy boat of their majority status—a boat I cannot get into because I am not white. The river, our societal mainstream, is accepted and hardly noticed. I manage to swim or float alongside the boat as I am learning how to navigate this mainstream. Every once in a while someone in the boat notices my struggle and tosses out an inner tube or briefly holds my hand. And then sometimes, someone reaches out and pushes my head under with, 'Just get over this race thing, Jean.' I sputter, resurface and continue on. In the long run, I figure it makes sense to construct a raft for myself. So while I talk to those in the boat and we run difficult rapids together, at the same time I must lash together whatever supportive materials I can find. The response? 'Hey, how come Jean gets a raft?' If I say, 'Because I can't get in the boat with you and I'm getting tired of staying afloat without more support.' Some of them say, 'What boat?'"

We all struggle with the complex issues raised by this metaphor, whether it applies to race or other areas of difference. The challenge for those in the water and for those in the boat is to reach out for each other on our common journey while aiming to make a difference in the very river that carries us all along.

May you have many wonderful experiences as you work to make a difference in your world this year.

A longer version of this 2003 commencement address to Oregon State University graduates appears in Jean's book, **Cultural Competence** *(Cengage Learning). See next page.*

"Detroit Lake"

"Sunset"

"Flooded Fields"

"Sunrays"

Please visit Jean Moule or order prints of her art at www.jeanmoule.com.

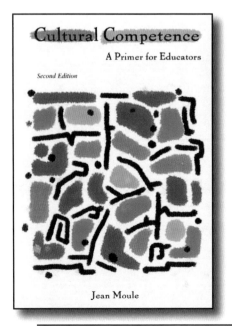

Cultural Competence: *A Primer for Educators, 2nd ed.,* by Dr. Jean Moule *(Wadsworth/Cengage Learning, 2012)* is a basic textbook for people in education. It opens pathways for effective and competent cross-cultural teaching. It presents a clear understanding of how a complex variety of social and psychological factors come together to shape a teacher's ability to work with K-12 students from a variety of cultures. The book initiates a process of learning that will ultimately lead you toward greater cultural competence as a teacher. Included are chapters on cultural competence, racism, culture, ethnocentricity and privilege, ethnic and biracial children, parenting, and families, bias in curriculum delivery and the practical dynamics of getting started. In addition, there are chapters focusing specifically on working with African Americans, Latinos, Asian Pacific Americans, Muslims, and American Indian/Alaskan Natives as well as a chapter on European Americans. Jean interviewed experts from these communities to write the book. Supporting forms and extended material available on companion website. 384 pages. ISBN 13-978-0-495-91529-4. www.cengagebrain.com